PRIMER contents

PAGE 2 — **Introduction - Tools for the Task**
David Shaw
Our editor introduces the issue, articles and contributors

PAGE 6 — **Life in a Foreign Country**
Ed Shaw
Understanding our changing culture

PAGE 16 — **Something Old - To Die For?**
Pete Sanlon
Sex and power in Michael Foucault's *The History of Sexuality*

PAGE 26 — **The Music and the Meaning of Male & Female**
Alastair Roberts
Tuning in to the theology of gender in Genesis 1 & 2

PAGE 44 — **No Longer Taboo**
Sam Allberry
Reflections and resources on the homosexuality debate

PAGE 54 — **Compassion Without Compromise**
Robert S. Smith
A pastoral response to the transgender crisis

PAGE 66 — **The Doctor Will See You Now**
Peter Saunders
An interview about the medical side of things

PAGE 71 — **Finding Our Feet in Shifting Sands**
Sharon James
Gender identity in the classroom and the courtroom

PRIMER introduction

TOOLS FOR THE JOB, JOB FOR THE TASK

Gender and Sexuality. I don't think I will need to convince you of how vital it is for the church to think through these things afresh, but I do want to say something about how we have approached these issues in *Primer* and how you should approach reading this issue of *Primer*.

Our approach to these issues in *Primer*

In our cultural context, what you're about to read will seem terribly narrow. We will resist the notion that happiness and freedom are found in a self-constructed identity and sexual liberation. We will argue from Scripture that God's vision for marriage is the faithful union of a man and a woman and we will argue that we are constituted men and women by virtue of our biology and not our feelings.

On the other hand, I want to draw your attention to two ways in which our approach is intentionally broad.

First, we have chosen to combine the issues of sexuality and gender. You'll find articles here that combine them or which address one or other of those topics. This is not to imply they are the same issue, despite the fact that they have been closely aligned in the acronym LGBT (Lesbian, Gay, Bisexual, Transgender). That said, there are good reasons to combine them. Biblically, both homosexuality and transgenderism reflect a world out of sync with God's creation design for men and women. Culturally, both of these movements argue from similar presuppositions about identity and freedom, and make common cause against what they see as oppressive and harmful traditional moral categories and social structures.

Second, you will find here articles that touch on a broad range of disciplines. We will trace the cultural and philosophical history of the LGBT movement (with help from Ed Shaw and Peter Sanlon). In the articles by Alastair Roberts, Sam Allberry, and Rob Smith we will explore the biblical material and how it is being interpreted today. And finally Peter Saunders and Sharon James write from medical, public policy and educational perspectives.

> One popular way of capturing the difference is to say that sexuality (LGB) defines who we want to go bed *with*, whereas gender (T) relates to who we go to bed *as*. The acronym inevitably continues to expand because it reflects a movement that wants to self-define and is suspicious of imposed or inherited categories, hence LGBTQQIAAP (Lesbian, Gay, Bisexual, Transgender, Queer, Questioning, Intersex, Asexual, Allies (a straight person who supports the cause) and Pansexual.

This breadth is crucial if we are to meet the pastoral challenges of the day. We will need to be familiar with what is taught in schools and what is caught in the cultural air we breathe if we are going to help people to disentangle themselves from the world and rejoice in God's ways. As we inevitably meet more serious brokenness and mess in the life of the church and our communities we will need to reflect carefully on the medical, social, theological and cultural aspects of any individual situation.

More broadly, it is crucial that we recognise the complexity of the pastoral task and draw on those various disciplines in appropriate measure. That complexity arises from the need to calibrate our response for several quite different audiences.

On the one hand there is the cultural campaign to champion sexual and gender freedoms, promoting itself as a moral crusade against oppressive forces like, well, traditional Christian morality. Given that this is almost permanently on the airwaves it's right to address it. We need to expose the harmfulness of what is promoted as health and the slavery of what is called freedom.

But we also need to have something to say to at least three other groups which will require a different tone and a different blend of those disciplines:

- One small but vital group are those who are born with intersex conditions. Their circumstances are frequently seized upon as evidence that the male/female binary is inadequate, and their experience is greatly trivialised by people who now identify themselves as 'intersex' simply to signal that they choose not to identify with the male or female binary.

- Another group are those who experience a profound difficulty living consistently with the gender (masculinity or femininity) that arises from their biological sex (i.e. those who would typically be diagnosed with 'gender dysphoria.') or those who experience same-sex attraction.

Of course some in these groups will be enlisted in the cultural campaign, but by no means all or many of them. Indeed, to some degree that cultural campaign nurtures and feeds upon these groups, and so we need to be willing to stand in the gap, offering a more compelling vision of where satisfaction and a secure identity are to be found.

- A final group to address a response are the wider public. They have no great cultural project they are pursuing, but they feel the appeal of the arguments that champion people's freedom to love who they want to love and be what they want to be.

When we reckon with this complexity, it becomes clear there is no one-size-fits-all answer. Yet we hope the breadth of articles here will equip you to proclaim the truth in your context and apply it with sensitivity.

How to approach this issue of *Primer*

The first thing to mention here arises from what we just said. Some of the articles that follow address the prevailing ideology and so will be more critical, deconstructing the lies and reconstructing a better vision for life in God's world. Other articles will have a more pastoral tone or focus as they reflect on how we help individuals understand themselves in light of God's word and live in its light. That is to say, there are different tools for different tasks here.

In addition though, we all need to recognise that some of us by temperament and experience will feel more at home tearing down secular ideologies, others of us asserting biblical truth and still others emphasising pastoral complexity and compassion. It is worth being alert to that as you read. Some articles will resonate more with you than others and you may gravitate towards them. Speaking for myself, though, I think I've learned the most from the articles which challenge my default settings. I hope that you find that to be true, and that you find this whole issue of *Primer*, taken together, to be a help.

DAVID SHAW is the Editor of *Primer*. He is part-time Theological Adviser for FIEC and part-time lecturer in New Testament and Greek at Oak Hill Theological College, London. He's married to Jo and they have four children.

 @_david_shaw

PRIMER contributors

SAM ALLBERRY is a pastor based at St Mary's Church in Maidenhead, Berkshire. He is a speaker for the Zacharias Trust, an editor for The Gospel Coalition, and the author of a number of books including *Is God Anti-Gay?* and *Why Bother With Church?*

 @SamAllberry

SHARON JAMES works for The Christian Institute, is the author of a number of books, and has spoken at conferences in many parts of the world. She studied History at Cambridge University, Theology at Toronto Baptist Seminary, and has a doctorate from the University of Wales.

ALASTAIR ROBERTS recently completed doctoral studies at Durham University. He is currently writing a book on the theology of the sexes for Crossway. He is a member of the *Mere Fidelity* podcast and a contributing editor to the *Political Theology Today* blog.

PETE SANLON is Vicar of St. Mark's Tunbridge Wells. He has a PhD from Cambridge University on *Augustine's Preaching* and has published several books on doctrine and culture, including *Plastic People: How Queer Theory Changes Us All*.

 @sanlon

PETER SAUNDERS trained as a General Surgeon before serving with the Africa Inland Mission in Kenya. Since 1992 he has served with the Christian Medical Fellowship, first as Head of Student Ministries and since 1999 as Chief Executive.

 @drpetersaunders

ED SHAW is the pastor of Emmanuel City Centre in Bristol and part of the editorial team at *livingout.org*. He loves his family and friends, church and city, gin and tonic, music and books. He is the author of *The Plausibility Problem: The church and same-sex attraction*.

ROBERT S. SMITH is an Anglican minister and theologian. He lectures in systematic theology and ethics at Sydney Missionary and Bible College, Australia and assists with ministry training and development in the Diocese of Sydney.

LIFE IN A FOREIGN COUNTRY

Ed Shaw helps us to understand our changing culture

Demonstration in London, November 1975

WHERE ARE WE?

L.P. Hartley's novel *The Go-Between* famously begins with the words: *"The past is a foreign country: they do things differently there."* But for many Christians today it's not the past that is the unfamiliar territory but the present. When it comes to defining and expressing gender, sexuality and marriage we'd be more at home with the language and culture of previous generations than with our western contemporaries; we often feel like complete strangers in a brave new world.

L P Hartley, *The Go-Between* (Harmondsworth: Penguin, 1958), 7.

The inevitable result is a nostalgia for the past that has too often stopped us from engaging and appreciating the ever-changing culture we live in. It has left us largely ineffective at articulating the timeless truths on gender, sexuality and marriage that God's perfect word contains and our imperfect world so needs. This article seeks to focus our attention on what exactly has changed – and why – so that we can get our bearings and start positively "speaking the truth in love" in ways that can be heard today. It will close by taking some first small steps in that direction.

life in a foreign country

WHAT'S CHANGED?

In a word: everything! Our legal system – once used to persecute the gay community – is now being used to prosecute Christians who've refused services to gay customers. The fear of coming out as an evangelical Christian in the workplace today is perhaps similar to the fear of coming out as gay to colleagues a generation ago. Dictionaries are having to change their definitions of words like 'marriage' and councils are asking the parents of young boys and girls to indicate their child's preferred gender identity. More and more young people talk of a fluidity in their experience of both gender and sexuality – rather than espousing the binary models that people used to fiercely cling to. Everything has changed – and at a bewildering speed.

Now it is important for us to recognise and articulate that not all the changes have been bad: the past is not necessarily a better country. The law criminalising consensual homosexual sex between adults was cruelly enforced. Hateful language was wrongly used to exclude and belittle people because of their sexual orientation. Too many young women and men have struggled in silence with big questions about their failure to fit into unhelpful gender stereotypes. We should be rejoicing at the end of: state-sponsored persecution of the gay community; the social acceptability of homophobic bullying; and nothing but an all-pervasive sound of silence on issues we all need compassionate support and guidance on.

But we also need to recognise that it is not good that the Bible's timeless teaching on gender, sexuality and marriage has been largely rejected by society – and increasing numbers within the church. Our Creator God's word is good and what it encourages or rules out is for our flourishing as his image-bearers. So when sexual activity is restricted to the lifelong marital relationship of a man to a woman that is for all our benefit. When we are told that women and men are different – and that those embodied differences matter in defining gender and who you can marry – that advice is kind not cruel. Not all the recent changes have been good for us and that reality needs to be shared.

But it needs to be shared by people who can answer this question:

WHERE HAVE THE CHANGES COME FROM?

The pace of social change has been so great that our focus has often just been on keeping up or resisting what we can. We've had very little time to analyse what factors have been powering the changes and what might be good and bad about them. We've got lost in the fog of our sub-culture's own nostalgia and failed to pay enough attention to what is creating the new weather conditions in the culture at large. We are therefore failing at our task of communicating God's wonderful truth to a world that desperately needs to hear it.

So where have the changes in our understanding of gender, sexuality and marriage come from? A whole number of directions, but I would like to share just a few key factors that come up again and again in the literature – and in everyday conversations. Our culture has changed because of:

1) What we regret

Change has been driven by what society regrets. People have recently woken up to the horrors of many attitudes and actions towards gay people in the past. Genuine homophobia was once all pervasive: "the fear or dislike of someone who identifies as lesbian or gay." Such fears and dislike (even hatred) ruled the majority's attitudes towards people perceived and portrayed as different to them (though it is important not to ignore the historic examples of kindness and understanding that can be found). Recent films like *The Imitation Game* have highlighted the shame and pain a gay man like the mathematician Alan Turing was put through in the 1950s to "cure" him of his homosexuality. Our society today rightly regrets such cruelties committed in the past and these regrets have powered many recent changes in law and practice.

www.stonewall.org.uk/help-advice/glossary-terms

Such changes in societal attitudes can be traced back not just to the wider sexual liberation of the mid-1960s but further back to the late 1950s: the ground-breaking Wolfenden Report was published in 1957 and recommended the decriminalisation of adult homosexual sexual activity (a full decade before this reached the English statute book). But the 1980s and the AIDS epidemic turned out to be a key turning point in bringing about societal repentance. Andrew Sullivan – a gay journalist living and working in the States – has written of his own personal experience of this time:

Andrew Sullivan, *Love Undetectable: reflections on friendship, sex and survival* (London: Vintage, 1999), 21.

AIDS dramatically altered the cultural strength of homophobia. By visiting young death upon so many, it ripped apart the notion of subterranean inviolability that forms such a powerful part of the fear of homosexuals. It need not have happened that way, of course. The notion that AIDS was divine punishment might have gained a wider consensus. The possibility of a mass quarantine, of forced ghettoization, of intensified stigma could have turned the epidemic into a terrifying reinforcement of homosexual otherness. But as tens of thousands of sons and uncles and brothers and fathers wasted away in the heart of America, something somewhat different happened. The image of secretive power that homosexuals allegedly held melted into a surprised form of shock and empathy. For some the old hatreds endured, of course, but for others an unsought-for and subtle transformation began to take shape. What had once been a strong fear of homosexual difference, disguising mostly silent awareness of homosexual humanity, became reversed. The humanity soon trumped the difference. Death, it turned out, was a powerfully universalizing experience. Suddenly, acquiescence in gay baiting and gay bashing became, even in its strongholds, something inappropriate at a moment of tragedy. The victimization by a disease ironically undercut their victimization by a culture. There was no longer a need to kick them when they were already down.

life in a foreign country

I think he is largely correct in his analysis. Genuine homophobia did not disappear overnight (it is sadly still present in many human hearts) but its cultural power was massively diminished by the AIDS epidemic – and has since been increasingly banished from public discourse. People were rightly moved by the severe suffering of the gay community and hugely impressed by how they loved and cared for their dying members – both strangers and friends. Massive societal changes in attitudes to other previously hated groups has often happened in response to them experiencing acute periods of suffering. The example of post-Holocaust changes in attitudes towards the Jews is one that Sullivan controversially draws upon as he portrays the similar effect he thinks the AIDS epidemic had on people's attitudes towards the gay community. It took the death of millions of Jews to wake people up to the cruel reality of anti-Semitism. He argues that it sadly took the death of countless gay people to wake us up to the cruelty of homophobia. His (admittedly controversial) point is that post-Holocaust western support for the founding of the nation of Israel can be compared to post-AIDS epidemic support for gay rights throughout the west. Some may argue that he overstates his case – but all of us need to recognise that such significant changes are so often driven by what we regret.

However, such right feelings of regret are clearly not enough to account for how much has changed – and how quickly. We also need to pay attention to changes in:

2) How we determine what is good

Changes in how we do our ethical thinking and decision-making are key to understanding changes in attitudes to same-sex sexual relationships in particular. On this a genuine must-read is American psychologist Jonathan Haidt's *The Righteous Mind: Why Good People are Divided by Politics and Religion*. In this best-selling book Haidt argues that the factors most important in determining what we think is right and wrong have changed significantly in recent decades and are now the things that most significantly divide conservative religious believers from their liberal secular neighbours. To illustrate this he has drawn up this helpful matrix:

Jonathan Haidt, The Righteous Mind: Why Good People are Divided by Politics and Religion (London: Penguin, 2012), 351.

The moral matrix of American liberals

#		
1.	care	harm
2.	liberty	oppression
3.	fairness	cheating
4.	loyalty	betrayal
5.	authority	subversion
6.	sanctity	degradation

In this matrix the numbers matter: the top three things are the most influential in determining the morality of a belief or behaviour for an American (or British) liberal. What they care about most is the avoidance of harm – if no one is harmed by an attitude or action how can it be wrong? Individual freedom of expression matters too and restrictions to this (other than those that prevent harm being done) are seen as oppressive. Fairness or equality is often appealed to and hypocrisy or cheating sniffed out wherever they can be found.

This leaves the bottom three factors much less influential to most of our contemporaries, but Haidt goes on to point out how they are often the most influential for religious believers. The moral matrix works, in many ways, in reverse order for us. Talk of sanctity or holiness and degradation or sin is regularly used in Christian ethics. The Bible is held up as our primary authority and attempts to reinterpret it are seen as subversive. Those who depart from traditional sexual ethics are seen as disloyal and barred from church leadership and membership due to their betrayal of community standards. We care most about very different things to our secular neighbours (though of course all of these factors matter to us all to some extent).

I think Haidt's matrix helps us get why our condemnation of permanent, faithful and stable same-sex sexual relationships gets no traction in our society today (especially with younger generations). Our friends and family question us: "Where is the harm in such a loving monogamous relationship? Is there not more harm in denying anyone that experience?" They exclaim: "How oppressive and unfair to say that there are some people who don't have the freedom to express themselves sexually! How hypocritical to talk about the beauty of sex within the marriage of a man and woman and then to deny that beauty to two men or two women!" And there is so much cultural power in such arguments isn't there? We feel it internally even as we seek to contradict it in an argument.

And there is so little cultural power in our regular responses as a result. Our replies focusing on God's definition of sin, the authority of his word, the need to be loyal to biblical standards, all fall on deaf ears because these concepts just aren't that important to many people anymore. We are speaking a language, appealing to values, they don't get – they are the ones using words and concepts that have the contemporary power to persuade.

life in a foreign country

This is even more the case because they understand much better than we do:

3) How we change our minds

The classic evangelical response to all of the above is to conclude that we need to teach people better – come up with more persuasive apologetic talks or sermons, add a seminar track on sexuality to the next weekend away or a question time after church one Sunday. Give people more information, the right information, and they will change their minds.

Tragically this response demonstrates that we just don't understand ourselves – how human beings today make their decisions. We are driven far more by our emotions than our intellects. This has been recognised in many other spheres: Drew Westen's *The Political Brain* has pointed out the role of powerful emotions rather than convincing arguments in determining American elections (the events of 2016 surely proving his point). Philosopher James K.A. Smith persuasively applies this sort of insight to the evangelical church:

Drew Westen, *The Political Brain: The role of emotion in deciding the fate of a nation* (Philadelphia: Public Affairs, 2008).

James KA Smith, *Desiring the Kingdom: Worship, Worldview, and Cultural Formation* (Grand Rapids: Baker, 2009), 76.

> ...I think we should first recognize and admit that the marketing industry – which promises an erotically charged transcendence through media that connects to our heart and imagination – is operating with a better, more creational, more incarnational, more holistic anthropology than much of the (evangelical) church. In other words, I think we must admit that the marketing industry is able to capture, form, and direct our desires precisely because it has rightly discerned that we are embodied, desiring creatures whose being-in-the-world is governed by the imagination. Marketers have figured out the way to our heart because they "get it": they rightly understand that, at root, we are erotic creatures – creatures who are orientated primarily by love and passion and desire. In sum, I think Victoria is in on Augustine's secret. But meanwhile the church has been duped by modernity and has bought into a kind of Cartesian model of the human person, wrongly presuming that the heady realm of ideas and beliefs is the core of our being. These are certainly part of being human, but I think they come second to embodied desire. And because of this, the church has been trying to counter the consumer formation of the heart by focusing on the head and missing the target: it's as if the church is pouring water on our head to put out the fire in our heart.

Let's flesh out what Smith is talking about in practice – and at a local church level. At best a young person in an evangelical church perhaps hears, once a year, a faithful, clear and intellectually persuasive articulation of the traditional Christian understanding of gender, sexuality and marriage. The rest of the year they are being bombarded by YouTube clips, soap operas, films and the rest that contradict that understanding and do so in beautifully appealing ways that engage them emotionally and visually – connecting with their desires. And that is how people change their minds today – the carefully prepared sex talk by the youth pastor is powerless against the expertly crafted short film. Just watch some and see. My experience is that these films best explain why young Christians are changing their minds on these issues – their wonderfully presented short narratives keep defeating what comes across as a dry – and rather long – legalistic set of rules from their church leaders. A few minutes on YouTube trumps years of biblical teaching because what the world offers connects with people's deepest desires for perfection, intimacy and beauty, and the church is just seen as denying people these things.

Two of the best examples would be Macklemore & Ryan Lewis' *Same Love* and Mike Buonaiuto's *Homecoming* (search for them on YouTube).

And we most definitely need to point the finger at ourselves rather than just the world around us. Because changes in attitudes to gender, sexuality and marriage are also being fuelled by:

4) What we worship

Everyone today worships sex. It's an idol both outside and inside the church: just think for a moment of the high pornography addiction levels you encounter everywhere today. The quest for sexual fulfilment drives us all at times. Christian anthropologist Jenell Williams Paris reflects on this all-pervasive idolatry:

Jenell Williams Paris, *The End of Sexual Identity: Why Sex Is Too Important to Define Who We Are* (Downers Grove: IVP, 2011), 112.

The idol of sexual fulfilment has two faces: One face says that each person has the right to be sexually satisfied and that having sex is a necessary part of happy, mature adulthood (or even adolescence). The second face is a Christian one that says the reward for premarital sexual virtue is great marital sex. When I was growing up, sexual ethics was all stick and no carrot: we were told to abstain from premarital sex because of the parental and divine punishment that would ensue. Today the stick is still there, but there's also a carrot: the less you sin before marriage, the hotter the sex after marriage.

life in a foreign country

In too many churches today the Christian sexual ethic of no sex before marriage is only being presented as the way to have better sex after marriage. We've just moderated society's obsession with sex by being obsessed by sex in its right context. So the sermon series on Song of Songs is all about the joys of marital sex with a few cautions to the youth group not to awaken their sexual desires before their wedding night (despite the fact that wider applications have been made throughout the rest of church history). This is not especially helpful to those same-sex attracted Christians we're saying should never have any sex at all. We too have started communicating that sexual fulfilment is essential to the good life when the one good life ever lived (that of the incarnate Christ) proves this wrong. But when sex has become everything, to deny it to anyone is seen as impossible and the push to change the church's traditional teaching becomes stronger and harder to resist. Sex used not to be seen as a human right; it is increasingly seen as that both outside and inside our churches.

WHAT CAN WE DO?

Change *ourselves*. Not biblical truths on gender, sexuality and marriage but how we incarnate and communicate them today:

- We need to keep apologising for the genuine homophobia of the past (and present) and show that we regret it too. In particular we would do well to say sorry to the gay community for how the church (largely) walked by on the other side of the road as they died in their thousands.

For notable exceptions see: *www.patheos.com/blogs/adrianwarnock/2014/06/aids-and-the-evangelical-a-case-study-in-compassion-and-social-justice/*

- We'll have to work hard at using all parts of Haidt's moral matrix – not just the categories we are most comfortable with – so that we can help our contemporaries hear God's good word. So if, for example, we're speaking into debates around sex change operations, let's be talking more of the potential harm it does than just what we think the Bible says.

- The Bible's great narrative of how gender, sexuality and marriage are all pointing us to God's love for us in Christ needs to be better connected to our God-given desires for perfection, intimacy and beauty. I recently heard of a large youth conference where this was done by acting out a marriage service for the young people and explaining each part's eternal symbolic significance in this powerfully emotional and visual way. The conference organisers had clearly grasped how hearts and minds are changed.

> Our idolatry of sex needs to be confessed and a vision of life to the full without it communicated. Our churches need to be places where people's singleness is valued and celebrated as much as people's marriages and where as much effort goes into encouraging intimate friendships as well as strong marriages.

It's not just society around us that needs to change – it's us too. My church and your church too.

SO WHERE DOES THAT LEAVE US?

Living in a foreign country. But all is not lost. Indeed if we get our cultural bearings we'll start making good gospel connections again. And that might not be as hard as it looks because, as author Ferdinand Mount reminds us, we've been here before:

Ferdinand Mount, *Full Circle: How the Classical World Came Back to Us* (London: Simon & Schuster: 2010), 1.

> *God's long funeral is over, and we are back where we started. Two thousand years of history have melted into the back story that no-one reads any more. We have returned to Year Zero, AD 0, or rather 0 CE, because we are in the Common Era now, the years of our Lord having expired.*
>
> *So much about society that is now emerging bears an astonishing resemblance to the most prominent features of what we call the classical world – its institutions, its priorities, its recreations, its physics, its sexual morality, its food, its politics, even its religion. Often without our being in the least aware of it, the ways in which we live our rich and varied lives correspond, almost eerily so, to the ways in which the Greeks and Romans lived theirs. Whether we are eating and drinking, bathing or exercising or making love, pondering, admiring or enquiring, our habits of thought and action, our diversions and concentrations recall theirs. It is as though the 1,500 years after the fall of Rome had been time out from traditional ways of being human.*

In many ways we have come full circle. Although that might depress us it should actually fill us with hope because it means that the church has faced many of these challenges before and grown despite them. The present might not be so foreign to us after all.

At the church I serve we've recently preached through the first half of 1 Corinthians and have found that the famous journey back to Corinth is much shorter than it used to be. The pastoral issues Paul was dealing with, and the cultural context he was speaking into, feel so familiar and his words are so easily applicable to the Britain of today. We have not been left without the help we need to proclaim the gospel afresh in this generation – whatever massive changes have taken place. **p**

life in a foreign country

PRIMER something old

"...the kind of pleasure I would consider as the real pleasure would be so deep, so intense, so overwhelming that I couldn't survive it. I would die."
Michel Foucault (1926 – 1984)

To Die For?

Sex and Power in Michel Foucault's *The History of Sexuality*
Introduced and annotated by Pete Sanlon

Introduction

Michel Foucault (1926-84) was a brilliant and troubled French scholar. As a fellow of the prestigious Collège de France, Foucault was free to read, teach and publish in ways that challenged the orthodoxies of centuries and set the scene for sexual re-inventions that are still being worked out today.

The chair Foucault held was named the professorship of 'History of Systems of Thought.' Foucault studied history not with a view to technical accuracy or detailed chronology, but rather to plunder it for insights that would foster liberation in his own life and culture. So he sought to write what he called a 'History of the Present' by unearthing the 'archaeology' of institutions, assumptions, beliefs and relationships. Previous philosophers had sought to change their culture by appealing to universal concepts, but Foucault sought to demonstrate that cultures and their institutions (such as hospitals, prisons and schools) are not founded in timeless principles of care or justice but are shaped by their assumptions which evolved over the centuries.

Two important features of these cultural assumptions were constantly highlighted by him. Firstly, the assumptions were developed as tools used to exercise power over people. In a very real sense Foucault believed that they imprison a person. The process of imposing expectations on people was begun in institutions such as prisons and asylums, then spreading in more subtle ways to the culture in general. Foucault called this process 'normalisation.' Encouraging liberation of the self from external expectations was thus a major goal of Foucault's ethics. Secondly, Foucault highlighted the ways that the assumptions could (and did) change, precisely because they were just exercises of power designed for particular moments.

In the final decade of his life Foucault turned to consider sexuality. The resulting three-volume work *The History of Sexuality* applied this approach to human sexuality.

Foucault considered the way modern assumptions about sex were shaped by ancient beliefs and practices. He saw in the ancient Greek and Roman world an approach to sex that was aware of dangers to life posed by excess and lack of control, but which nevertheless embraced a wide range of approaches to sex as beneficial and virtuous. In contrast to this, Foucault saw a more negative view of sex in ancient Christianity, filled with dire warnings about indwelling sin and the flesh itself.

Foucault sought to demonstrate that as the centuries progressed, the interaction of these sexual ethics produced a powerful cultural narrative about sex in his day. In particular, his focus was upon the way in which a whole network of taboos and expectations exerted power over people. The power so exercised was rarely recognised such that people are like puppets pulled about by strings they could not see. Foucault's response to all this was to commend a vision of ethics as 'self-transformation' or 'care of the self.' Once a person realises how much their sexual identity and preferences are nothing more than submission to power exerted over them, they can engage on the lifelong journey of liberating themselves from such power.

For that reason Foucault refused to sign up with any movement or institution – he rejected the homosexual and feminist movements as he did the Church and government. Nevertheless his writings were immensely significant in shaping the assumptions of a generation that is suspicious of power and wants to believe that sexual desires, identity and practice are entirely fluid and culturally conditioned. Whether people realise it or not, today's idea that our sexuality or gender can be changed at will in pursuit of liberation and satisfaction is nothing more than a living out of Foucault's philosophy. Foucault himself sought to live out his creed – homosexuality, sadomasochism, drugs, suicide attempts – he longed to experience pleasure and what he called 'limit experiences.' Eventually dying of AIDs aged 57, his personal life remains a much written about enigma, prophecy and parable for a culture that seeks infinite freedom apart from the infinite God.

By now it should be clear how relevant Foucault is to our culture today. He is not an easy read though! His style is very dense, so we have chosen quite a short excerpt from *The History of Sexuality*. The aim isn't necessarily to understand every phrase or sentence, but to follow the overall argument and feel its remarkable force. To help make sense of his argument we need to understand how he defines two key terms: "sex" and "sexuality." Throughout this passage, "sexuality" is the basic and uninterpreted experience of pleasure and the longing for it. "Sex" on the other hand, is the cultural interpretation layered upon these pleasures and longings. It is the whole network of cultural expectations imposed upon people by codes of behaviour in society, church, families and education. The idea of "sex" is therefore a bad thing; it is a fictitious application of power that manipulates us with its promise of acceptance, virtue and self-realisation. Keeping those different meanings in mind as you read is vital.

At the point we join the argument, Foucault has just argued that 19th century society demonised sexual acts by linking them with mental illness, and the Roman Catholic Church did the same by forbidding contraception and so driving people to interrupt intercourse as a form of natural contraception. In these areas and others, Foucault saw society as imposing taboos and expectations that created the concept of sex and restricted an individual's freedom to access their true selves. He now describes why that network of taboos and expectations was so effective in exerting power over people.

```
The following excerpt is taken from The History of Sexuality Volume 1: An Introduction by Michel
Foucault, translated by Robert Hurley (Allen Lane 1979, first published as 'La Volonte de savoir'
1976). Copyright © Editions Gallimard, 1976. Translation copyright © Random House, Inc., 1978,
pages 154-57. Reproduced by permission of Penguin Books Ltd.
```

The History of Sexuality

The theory thus generated performed a certain number of functions that made it indispensable. First, the notion of "sex" made it possible to group together, in an artificial unity, anatomical elements, biological functions, conducts, sensations, and pleasures, and it enabled one to make use of this fictitious unity as a causal principle, an omnipresent meaning, a secret to be discovered everywhere: sex was thus able to function as a unique signifier and as a universal signified.

Foucault's first point is that the whole network of expectations and assumptions that make up the "notion of 'sex'" become the dominant way people understand their lives and relationships to others. For Foucault, identities such as transsexual, homosexual, husband, celibate, etc. would all be examples of artificially constructed roles imposed on people and accepted by them. Chosen rather than discovered, they are artificial. While many today think their identity as homosexual or transgender must, in some way, be rooted in biology or genes, Foucault viewed this as an artificial and imprisoning interpretation. The culture promises an all-encompassing explanation of who we are, but that explanation enslaves us with the expectations it brings. So Foucault would explain the contemporary obsession with sexual fulfilment as an artificially created search for gold at the end of a rainbow. For Foucault, ultimate liberation and self-knowledge requires that one see past their constricting and false meanings.

Further, by presenting itself in a unitary fashion, as anatomy and lack, as function and latency, as instinct and meaning, it was able to mark the line of contact between a knowledge of human sexuality and the biological sciences of reproduction; thus, without really borrowing anything from these sciences, excepting a few doubtful analogies, the knowledge of sexuality gained through proximity a guarantee of quasi-scientificity; but by virtue of this same proximity, some of the contents of biology and physiology were able to serve as a principle of normality for human sexuality...

By expressing our artificial visions of sex in scientific language we legitimate the lifestyles concerned. We see this today when the media prefaces articles which commend a sexual lifestyle with an impartial 'survey' of people's views or we read that many 'scientists' believe in something or another. All this Foucault would say is a manipulative effort to ensure we do not break free from the expectations society would impose upon us.

There is a symbiotic relationship between science and sex. Not only does use of scientific terms lend artificial sexual identities legitimacy, also the use of scientific terms gives those terms an ever greater power over details of our lives. The more 'surveys' are used to justify acceptance of a particular sexual lifestyle, the more authority and power they gain. People begin to think that if a survey or scientific view has not validated them then they are abnormal.

something old --- *to die for?*

...It might be added that "sex" performs yet another function that runs through and sustains the ones we have just examined. Its role in this instance is more practical than theoretical. It is through sex – in fact, an imaginary point determined by the deployment of sexuality – that each individual has to pass in order to have access to his own intelligibility (seeing that it is both the hidden aspect and the generative principle of meaning), to the whole of his body (since it is a real and threatened part of it, while symbolically constituting the whole), to his identity (since it joins the force of a drive to the singularity of a history).

This paragraph expresses so well the power of "sex" in our culture. It has become such a dominant aspect of people's lives that it controls how they seek to understand themselves, how they relate to their bodies and how they cultivate a sense of identity. For Foucault, a certain degree of freedom and clarity can be achieved by recognising the ways sexual taboos and expectations create one's identity. But in Foucault's worldview this is never really attainable, since Foucault would argue that every step towards freedom from an expectation or taboo merely moves us into the embrace of another assumption which itself masks a power that controls us.

Some of Foucault's work analysed the way states (such as monarchies or early democracies) and institutions (such as prisons or asylums) exercise power over people. The state and institutions exercised what one could call 'hard' power over people. Foucault thought that as time moved on to the modern age, 'soft' power began to be exercised over all people via a myriad of subtle ways. For him, these were foreshadowed in early Christian pastoral practices that, in the arena of sex, urged people to resist the temptations of the flesh.

Through a reversal that doubtless had its surreptitious beginnings long ago – it was already making itself felt at the time of the Christian pastoral of the flesh – we have arrived at the point where we expect our intelligibility to come from what was for many centuries thought of as madness; the plenitude of our body from what was long considered its stigma and likened to a wound; our

Foucault noted that the Early Church had a theology and pastoral practice which formed the basis of Western civilisation. That theology of sin and the flesh as it was secularised by the Enlightenment saw sexual pleasure and excess as akin to madness. Foucault noted the irony that later modernity sought the very meaning of existence in sex. Meaning and ultimate satisfaction is sought in that which had previously been thought of as insanity.

identity from what was perceived as an obscure and nameless urge. Hence the importance we ascribe to it, the reverential fear with which we surround it, the care we take to know it. Hence the fact that over the centuries it has become more important than our soul, more important than our life, and so it is that all the world's enigmas appear frivolous to us compared to this secret, miniscule in each of us, but of a density that makes it more serious than any other.

> *Sex holds such promise to people that, as Foucault predicted, it replaced the soul as our chief concern in life and death. The years since Foucault's death have served only to accumulate further evidence that he was profoundly insightful at this point. The challenge of how a church can be a counter-cultural community that rehabilitates people to rightly understand and value the importance of their souls remains to be met.*

The Faustian pact, whose temptation has been instilled in us by the deployment of sexuality, is now as follows: to exchange life in its entirety for sex itself; for the truth and the sovereignty of sex. Sex is worth dying for. It is in this (strictly historical) sense that sex is indeed imbued with the death instinct. When a long while ago the West discovered love, it bestowed on it a value high enough to make death acceptable; nowadays it is sex that claims this equivalence, the highest of all. And while the deployment of sexuality permits the techniques of power to invest life, the fictitious point of sex, itself marked by that deployment, exerts enough charm of everyone for them to accept hearing the grumble of death within it...

> *Faust was the central character in a classic German play. As a dissatisfied scholar, Faust made a deal with the devil: in exchange for his soul he would be granted worldly pleasures and unlimited knowledge. It ends, needless to say, badly. One cannot help but reflect on our culture's prioritising of sex over the soul and hear the question of Jesus: "What can a person give in exchange for their soul?" (Mark 8:37)*

> *The Romantic Movement and Shakespearean aspirations taught society that romantic visions of love were worth dying for – most famously in the play Romeo and Juliet. Foucault quite correctly discerned that the infinite value placed on romantic love in past days is now sought more specifically in sexual identities and acts. For Foucault there is no freedom to be found in this shift because, in his view, sex simply represents a different form of the very same power exerted over people.*

> *We have a fearful suspicion that sex is not enough to satisfy longing for eternity. The promises made to us via the cultural codes of sexual expectations are never quite enough to assure us of victory over, or significance in the light of, our mortality. To some degree the Foucault-liberated person knows that the promises sex makes cannot deliver.*

...So we must not refer a history of sexuality to the agency of sex; but rather show how "sex" is historically subordinate to sexuality. We must not place sex on the side of reality, and sexuality on that of confused ideas and illusions; sexuality is a very real historical formation; it is what gave rise to the notion of sex, as a speculative element necessary to its operation.

Foucault is now describing what we must do. The first is to realise that "sexuality" is primary, and that the whole network of expectations that make up "sex" are secondary. In the next paragraph, he urges his readers to make a break from those expectations ("sex") and prioritise bare emotions and acts ("sexuality").

Again Foucault makes the point: the human who longs for some form of sex is unaware of the ways he or she is being manipulated and overwhelmed by the power of cultural interpretations layered upon his or her more basic sexual longings.

We must not think that by saying yes to sex, one says no to power; on the contrary, one tracks along the course laid out by the general deployment of sexuality. It is the agency of sex that we must break away from, if we aim – through a tactical reversal of the various mechanisms of sexuality – to counter the grips of power with the claims of bodies, pleasures and knowledges, in their multiplicity and their possibility of resistance. The rallying point for the counterattack against the deployment of sexuality ought not to be sex-desire, but bodies and pleasures.

For Foucault, pleasure is simply to be found in intense experience. As he once said, "the kind of pleasure I would consider as the real pleasure... would be so deep, so intense, so overwhelming that I couldn't survive it. I would die. I'll give you a clearer and simpler example. Once I was struck by a car in the street. I was walking. And for maybe two seconds I had the impression that I was dying and it was really a very, very intense pleasure. The weather was wonderful. It was seven o'clock during the summer. The sun was descending. The sky was very wonderful and blue and so on. It was, it still is now, one of my best memories."

Recorded in James Miller, *The Passion of Michel Foucault* (Cambridge, Mass.: Harvard University Press, 2000), 306.

The front at which Foucault calls people to fight is the point at which culture oppresses us with its interpretations of sexuality. When all labels, orientations, desires and expectations for the virtuous practice of sex are rejected – all that remains is bodies that seek pleasures. Any words beyond that – even interpretations that say one is free to engage in the practice – will in fact just exert power and oppress.

Conclusion

The formative influence on Foucault's early thinking was reading the arch-atheist, Nietzsche. A bold embrace of atheism drove Foucault to understand the world with no possibility of an authoritative external interpretation from the Creator. As he explored history, Foucault realised that the assumptions and institutions which many thought timeless and universal were actually changeable and contingent on culture. Some of the insights Foucault developed can be welcomed by Christians – others are challenged by the gospel.

To begin with, we can welcome Foucault's realisation that behind many institutions and assumptions lie dark aspirations to exert power over others. Many a Christian organisation or church has had to face the painful reality of power being abused. We are called to lead and preach in a way that has a different view of power to the culture around us (Mark 10:42-44, 2 Cor 4:2). Foucault was suspicious of people's ability to abuse power and when doing so to hide behind moral and institutional authority. Those of us who know the power of sin in our hearts share Foucault's suspicion of power.

Christians can also accept much of Foucault's critique of the assumption that institutions and values always remain constant or hold universal authority. In reality much that people value is neither universal nor timeless – we are all creatures of our culture and times far more than we will admit. Believers are called to be missionaries to our generation and so we must be wise and sacrificial in setting aside personal preferences for the sake of the lost (1 Cor 9:19-22). That said, in God's word we have the authoritative word from our Creator and Saviour and so we are sent as missionaries to our culture with his blueprint for life with him and one another. By our example and our teaching we need to show that that blueprint is not oppressive but is where we gain definitive access to our identities and the purposes of our bodies.

Foucault's insights about the danger of power and the reality of change in this world are salutary. Ironically though, they don't just challenge the believer who sees connections with scriptural warnings. They also ought to challenge the secular culture that has embraced Foucault's ethic of self-invention and sexual fluidity. Does Foucault's critique regarding power and change not apply equally to his own ethic and his contemporary followers? Behind today's culture of sexual diversity and liberation lurks some of the most extensive and totalitarian claims to power made in the history of Western civilisation – people lose their jobs on the basis of social media posts, online shaming occurs on an international scale, employers and judges enforce diversity codes, children are evaluated by government agencies – the list could go on. Foucault challenges those who liberate sex to ponder why so many threats and restrictions are necessary to usher in their dreams of freedom.

Furthermore, Foucault's reflections on the changeability of cultural assumptions challenge the sexual liberation movement. If all moral codes and institutions have developed in a genealogical fashion, must this not also be true of our late-modern sexual liberation culture? Will people in centuries to come not look back on present moral certitudes regarding sexual diversity much as we look back on the 19th century's scientific, rational certainties regarding Western culture's superiority?

Christians will also wish to affirm Foucault's insistence that true philosophy and true knowledge must be appropriated into the individual's life. Foucault taught this and he lived it out. Much philosophy prior to Foucault had degenerated into what amounted to a branch of mathematics. It was a study irrelevant to daily life and obsessed with academic minutiae. Foucault restored the ancient vision of a philosopher as one profoundly concerned with how to live everyday life. In a certain way he models the combination of serious thought and lived-out reality. Far too many Christians imagine they know how to live at work, raise a family, lead a church or counsel the broken hearted on the basis of an article read online and without drinking deeply from the theological training previous generations valued. We have too many armchair leaders and backseat drivers. On the other hand, Foucault would say that academic knowledge that has not been appropriated (often with pain and suffering) into the depths of a life is simply not real knowledge. We do not know or understand that which we have not lived.

And yet there are crucial ways the gospel offers a better vantage point from which to challenge power – especially as regards sexual self-transformation. The spiritual power granted to Christians is that of the Holy Spirit, who brings not manipulation and deception but freedom and truth. We are not left to lurch endlessly from one experience of being under an imprisoning power to another, because the Saviour who has all power set his authority aside to die for us (Phil 2:6-8). His humble act of setting aside power opens up for his disciples the beautiful possibility that in our church relationships we can view and treat each other as he has treated us (Phil 2:5). Our church communities can become counter-cultural places of preferring the needs of others to ourselves. When people eventually see through the endless manipulations, deceptions and broken promises of the sexual liberation culture, they will need the healing power of a church. Foucault never found that resting place or satisfaction – will the people around us find it? P

Grayson Perry on sexual revolutions:

"SOMETIMES THESE REVOLUTIONS ARE PITCHED AS IF THEY'RE SOME KIND OF 'MORAL GOOD FORCE.' OFTEN, THEY'RE LIKE EXPLOSIONS THAT ARE THROWN INTO STABLE HOMES. THEY'RE VERY DISRUPTIVE FOR PEOPLE'S REAL, ORDINARY, 'NORMAL' LIVES."

On *The Andrew Marr Show*, BBC Radio 4, Mon 18th Feb 2013.

the music and the meaning of Male & Female

Alastair Roberts helps us to tune in to the theology of gender in Genesis 1 & 2

Introduction

Although the Scriptures address the topic of the sexes on many occasions, it is within the opening chapters of Genesis that its foundational treatment of the subject is to be discovered. That so much of the fundamental teaching on the subject of the sexes is contained within the first two chapters of the Bible is itself an initial indication of just how closely entwined this subject is with the scriptural narrative more generally, and how important a theme it must be for any theology that faithfully arises from it. The more closely we attend to the text of Genesis 1-2, the more apparent it will be that gendered themes are subtly diffused throughout.

Yet the foundation offered by Genesis 1-2 may initially appear unpromising in some respects. As a more literary and poetic narrative text, it does not present the same robust propositional statements that we find in such places as the Pauline epistles. Those searching for clear theological propositions may rummage around in the packing chips of narrative and come up with relatively little reward for their efforts. Not only do literary readings of narrative texts demand very sensitive and delicate forms of interpretation, they also seem much more vulnerable to contestation. Without definitive propositional statements, such passages seem considerably less serviceable for direct theological controversy, which has provoked the majority of the writing on this subject over the last couple of decades. The strength of a literary reading is seldom as straightforward as the strength of a logical argument. The former is incapable of forcefully securing assent: if and when it persuades, it does so through its elegance, fittingness, and attractiveness. To those who refuse to be persuaded and insist upon reading a text against its grain for their own purposes, it may present little challenge.

There are, however, advantages to building our theology upon such a foundation. As much of the theological teaching of Scripture is conveyed through subtle literary means, any approach that attends closely to narrative will be much more securely grounded. It also offers a considerably broader base than many doctrinal arguments, which depend upon a few heavy load-bearing texts for support. Such literary readings can expose the hidden root systems of biblical teachings in scriptural narratives, revealing how deeply embedded in the text certain claims are, and the impossibility of removing them without considerable violence. Although a theological case established upon such a literary reading may be lightly dismissed, it can only truly be answered by a more sensitive and attentive reading of the passages in question. It is precisely at this point, rather than in the clash of competing propositions and their arrayed battalions of proof-texts, that the weaknesses and flaws of unscriptural positions often emerge, as they fail to offer a compelling reading of the Scriptures in their breadth.

A literary reading must be alert to the use of metaphor, to subtle intertextual echoes, to the significance of narrative progressions and patterns, to characterisation, and other such factors. Much scriptural teaching on the sexes, as on other subjects, is conveyed through such artful literary means. Not every detail of such a reading is equally robustly supported by the text and some of my remarks in what follows may drift into more speculative readings of suggestive details. However, the accuracy and theological import of more salient points can be made more explicit by the presence of many supporting literary details throughout the passages in question, spreading the weight of the text's teaching, rather than focusing it entirely on a few proof-texts.

The Pattern of Creation in Genesis 1

The creation and blessing of man and woman in Genesis 1 is part of the wider creation narrative and ought to be viewed against that backcloth. In the course of six days God creates, structures, names, establishes generation, fills, and delegates rule over the heavens and the earth. These six days naturally divide into two halves, with the first three days and the second three days each involving different sorts of tasks, while corresponding to each other in their sequence.

Days one to three (verses 1-13) are days of structuring, division, taming, and naming. These creation days address the first problem with the original creation: that it is without form (cf. verse 2). On day one, God creates the light, divides light from darkness, and names them Day and Night. On day two, God creates the firmament, dividing the waters above from the waters below, and calls the firmament Heaven. On day three, God gathers together the waters, so that the dry land appears, dividing the one from the other. He calls the dry land Earth and the gathering of the waters he calls Seas. These days involve the establishment of stable regions with their boundaries.

Days four to six (verses 14-31) are days of generating, establishing succession, filling, glorifying, and establishing communion. On day four we return to the division of light from darkness and day from night, as God places the sun, moon, and stars in the firmament to provide light on the earth and to uphold the division of day from night. On day five, the waters above and below are populated as God empowers the waters to bring forth living creatures and causes birds to fly across the face of the firmament expanse. On day six, the earth – divided from the seas on the third day – is also empowered to bring forth living creatures. These three creation days answer the second problem with the original creation: that it is void. The 'heavens and the earth' that are structured on the first three days are populated with their 'host' in the second three days (2:1).

It is on this sixth day that mankind is created and given dominion over the fish of the sea, birds of the air, and the creatures of the earth. Mankind – male and female – is blessed and instructed to be fruitful, to multiply, to fill the earth, to subdue it, and to exercise dominion over its living creatures. There is a sort of progression implied here, as fertility and procreation gives rise to growth in population, which leads in turn to the spreading out of the human population upon the earth, which results in a steady taming and subduing of the natural wilderness, which, finally, establishes mankind's rule over all of the creatures of God's creation.

This progressive vocation has two key unifying themes: dominion (subdue and exercise dominion) and filling (be fruitful, multiply, and fill the earth). We should notice that these two themes correspond to the two stages of God's own creation work. Dominion relates to the first three days, where God divides, establishes, tames, and names the fundamental structures of creation. Filling relates to the second three days, where God generates new beings, fills, populates, glorifies, and establishes communion within his creation. Here we find an initial indication that humanity's vocation within the world is to reflect, continue, and to extend God's own creative rule of Genesis 1.

The Creation of Mankind

Mankind's creation is described in Gen 1:27 in a threefold parallelism:

A.	1) God created	2) man	3) in his image
B.	3) in the image of God	1) he created	2) him
C.	3) male and female	1) he created	2) them

There are a few things to observe about this parallelism, in which the second two statements unpack the first.

First, man has both singularity and plurality: man is first spoken of as a singular entity ('him'), then later as the plurality of male and female ('them'). Humanity has a number of aspects to it: humanity is a *kind*, a *race*, and a *multitude*. As a *kind*, humanity is a unique species that finds its source and pattern in the original human being created in the image of God. Humanity is a *race* on account of its possession of generative potential as male and female and its spread and relationship to its origins through such unions. Humanity is a *multitude* as it realises this potential and fills the earth.

the music and the meaning of male & female

Second, sexual difference is the one difference within humanity that is prominent in the creation narrative. This significance is not merely that it gestures towards the generic plurality of humanity. Rather, it is male and femaleness which renders us a race and establishes the primary bonds of our natural relations and source of our given identities. We have been empowered as male and female to bring forth new images of God and of ourselves (cf. Genesis 5:3) and are ordered towards each other in a much deeper way than just as individual members of a 'host'.

Third, there is widespread agreement among biblical scholars that the concept of the image of God in Genesis refers to a royal office or vocation that humanity enjoys within the world, as the administrator and symbol of God's rule. The image of God is primarily focused upon the dominion dimension of mankind's vocation. However, the filling dimension of mankind's vocation – to which the maleness and femaleness of humanity chiefly corresponds – is not unconnected to this, as in the third part of the parallelism 'male and female' is paralleled with the 'image of God' in the first two parts.

See, for instance, J. Richard Middleton, *The Liberating Image: The Imago Dei in Genesis 1* (Grand Rapids, MI: Brazos Press, 2005).

Thus, by the end of Genesis 1, there are already a number of key terms, patterns, and distinctions in play. In subsequent chapters, these are given clearer shape as they are unpacked and developed.

Genesis 1 & 2

Genesis 2 contains a repeat in miniature of the great creation narrative of chapter 1. Verse 4 begins a new section of the Genesis account, what many have termed a second creation account. While this account is often presented as if it were an alternative creation account to that of Genesis 1, there are close relations between the two. Perhaps the most striking is the manner in which Genesis 2 roughly follows the pattern of Genesis 1.

Genesis 1	Genesis 2
Day 0: Heaven and earth created. Earth formless and void and covered by a vast watery deep (1:2).	Heaven and earth created. Earth without plants and herbs of the field, or a man to till the ground. The earth originally irrigated by ground waters that come up from it and cover its entire face (2:4-6).
Day 1: Light created (1:3-5).	The *adam* created (2:7).
Day 2: Firmament created dividing the waters above from the waters beneath. Firmament named Heaven (1:6-8).	Garden created and divided from the rest of the world, a sanctuary model of heaven (2:8).
Day 3: Waters gathered together in Seas, revealing the dry land, Earth. Earth brings forth vegetation (1:9-13).	The ground waters are gathered together in rivers, which mark out distinct lands and enable them to be named. The garden filled with trees and vegetation (2:9-14).
Day 4: Lights placed in the firmament as signs to rule the day and night, to divide the light from the darkness, and to give light to the earth (1:14-19).	The *adam* placed in the firmament garden to serve and guard it, a sign of God's rule, dividing it from the rest of the world. He is given the law concerning the tree (2:15-17).
Days 5-6: Sea creatures, birds of the air, creatures of the land are brought forth by earth and sea, after which in an act of special and more direct creation, mankind is formed (1:20-28).	God forms beasts and birds from the ground, representing the creatures of days 5 and 6 and brings them to the *adam*, who names them but does not find a suitable mate. Finally, in a distinct act of creation, God creates the woman out of the man's side and brings her to him (2:18-23).
Day 7: God rests from his labours (2:1-3).	Man and woman naked and unashamed together in the garden (2:24-25).

> I have chosen to employ the terminology of 'the *adam*', rather than 'Adam'. Within Genesis 1-3, *adam* doesn't yet seem to function as a proper name, as it later does in places such as 4:25. Nor does *adam* mean 'man' (as *ish* does in 3:23), identifying the man over against the woman (*ishshah*). Rather, the term defines the man – the earthling – relative to the earth (*adamah*) from which he was formed. It is also the term used for the entire humankind. As the specific connotations and connections of such a term are an important dimension of its meaning, it can be helpful to alert ourselves to these when interpreting or translating a term such as *adam*.

In addition to repeating in miniature the creation pattern of Genesis 1, Genesis 2 also presents the establishment of the *adam* and the woman in the garden as a continuation of the narrative begun in the previous chapter. God rested on the seventh day, but, in contrast to the previous creation days, there is no reference to the end of the seventh day. Rather, the creation narrative of Genesis 2 is about the delegation of the creation to the charge of mankind: God's resting is bound up with the commissioning of humanity.

the music and the meaning of male & female

The creation that God delegates rule over to mankind is an incomplete creation. Outside of the Garden, the earth still needs to be subdued, filled, and named. God prepares the *adam* for this task by giving him a worked model and a period of apprenticeship in the Garden of Eden, a kindergarten for humanity in its infancy. In chapter 2, God charges the *adam* with working on a part of the creation that he had left unfinished, and oversees him in that task. Although God had named all of the regions established on the first three days, all of the creatures with which God had populated them remained unnamed. God brings these creatures to the *adam* in order that he might complete this part of the work of creation.

Although we may be inclined to think of the creation as if a static container packed with assorted contents, the creation narrative has a profoundly temporal structure. Evening and morning, day and night, seasons and years, a week of creation work divided into two distinct yet parallel halves, the repetition with variation of that pattern in the following chapter. The first two chapters of Genesis also present us with a creation that strains forward to realise its calling and purpose. Humanity must be fruitful and multiply. The earth must be tamed, named, and filled, and mankind must exercise dominion over its creatures. The gold and precious stones of Havilah (Gen 2:11-12) must be mined and the riches of other lands brought in to glorify the Garden, as mankind moves outward into the world. Man must mature in rule, subduing the wider creation. Rather than comparing it to a container being packed with contents, it might be more apt to understand the creation depicted in Genesis 1-2 as if the opening of a grand symphony, anticipating and propelling the listener into the richly orchestrated movement which follows.

This must be borne in mind when we read the Scriptures more generally, within which it becomes clear that the creation account is very much part of a broader narrative. Themes introduced in these chapters are developed, unfolded, and perfected. This is perhaps nowhere clearer than in Revelation, where in the new creation many of the themes of the first creation are revisited. Christ and his bride are joined together in a glorified Garden-City, into which the riches of the whole world have been brought, and from which a river of living water flows. Each of the divisions of the first three days is transformed: there is no longer night, for the everlasting Day has dawned (Revelation 21:23-25); there is no longer a firmament veil dividing heaven from earth (21:2-3); there is no more sea (21:1).

The temporal impulse of the creation narrative must also be kept at the forefront of our minds when reflecting upon the relation between male and female, who are created by God as characters in and agents of this larger narrative. The creation of man and woman is one of the ways in which God establishes, fulfils, and manifests his purpose in the mighty symphony of his creation. Man and woman, in their particular labour and relations, have a sort of 'musical' role to perform. They repeat in their own ways the foundational musical themes provided by God's own labour and provide figures of 'musical' realities that are gloriously expressed in Christ and the Church. The bringing together of man and woman in marriage and their bringing forth and raising of offspring also provides a sort of generational metre to human history. Finally, as we are caught up in a larger symphony of creation, realities such as marriage must be considered in terms of the purpose that they play within this. This is why, when the purpose of subduing and filling the creation and populating the earth in the face of death that marriage currently performs has been fulfilled, there will no longer be marrying or giving in marriage (Luke 20:34-38).

Differentiation in Humanity's Creation and Vocation

Whereas Genesis 1 focuses upon the creation, commissioning, and blessing of mankind in general and in an undifferentiated fashion, in Genesis 2 a more specific and differentiated view of male and female comes into view. It is important that we read Genesis 1 and 2 in close correspondence with each other for this reason.

That there should be gendered differentiation in the fulfilment of the divine commission is hardly surprising when we consider the tasks that lie at the heart of mankind's vocation. Although both sexes participate in both tasks, exercising dominion and being fruitful are not tasks that play to male and female capabilities in an equal manner, but rather are tasks where sexual differentiation is usually particularly pronounced. In the task of exercising dominion and subduing creation, the man is advantaged by reason of the male sex's typically significantly greater physical strength, resilience, and willingness to expose itself to risk. He is also advantaged on account of the greater social strength of bands of men. In the task of being fruitful, multiplying, and filling the creation, however, the most important capabilities belong to women. It is women who bear children, who play the primary role in nurturing them, and who play the chief role in establishing the communion that lies at the heart of human society. These are differences seen across human cultures.

As G.K. Beale has argued, the Garden of Eden is a divine sanctuary and there are many clues within Genesis 2 to this fact. In verse 15, the *adam* is placed in the Garden to cultivate and guard it, the same words that are repeatedly used to refer to the Israelites who are set apart to serve God and keep his word, or the priests who keep the service or charge of the tabernacle. God walks about in the midst of the Garden. The Garden is the site of holy food, some of which is forbidden. The *adam* is also given a law concerning the Tree of the Knowledge of Good and Evil, which he must uphold.

G.K. Beale, *The Temple and the Church's Mission: A Biblical Theology of the Dwelling Place of God* (Leicester: Apollos, 2004) 66ff.

One might surmise a gendered differentiation in relation to the human vocation in chapter 1. In the context of God's establishing the order of the sanctuary in chapter 2, and the outcome of the overturning of that order in chapter 3, such a gendered differentiation becomes more explicit, not least in the fact that the priestly task chiefly falls to the *adam*, rather than his wife.

the music and the meaning of male & female

There are a series of sharp and important contrasts between the *adam* and his companion, the woman, in Genesis 2:

First, and perhaps most obvious, the man is created before the woman (cf. 1 Corinthians 11:7-9 and 1 Timothy 2:13).

Second, the man alone can stand for humanity as a whole. In Genesis 2, the creation of mankind is not the creation of an undifferentiated population of people, but the creation of an *adam* from the *adamah*, followed by the later creation of a woman from the *adam*'s side. It is in this particular being that the human race finds its unity. This is a point borne out in the rest of Scripture: Adam is the representative head of the old humanity. This humanity is *Adamic* humanity, not *Adamic-Evean* humanity. Mankind is particularly summed up in the man.

Third, the image of God is especially focused upon the *adam*. He is the figure who peculiarly represents and symbolises God's dominion in the world. The *adam* is placed within the Garden as the light within its firmament (the lights on day four are established as rulers), charged with upholding the divisions that God had established, performing the royal function associated with the divine imaging. Like God, in his great dominion and subduing acts of the first three days of creation, the man names and orders the creatures.

Fourth, the *adam* is created to be a tiller and guardian of the earth, while the woman is created to be the helper of the *adam*, to address the multifaceted problem of his aloneness. The sort of help that the woman is expected to provide to the *adam* has been a matter of considerable debate. However, it isn't hard to discover the core of the answer. If it were for the naming of the animals, the task is already completed. If it were purely for the labour of tilling of the earth, a male helper would almost certainly be preferable. While men can undoubtedly find the companionship of women very pleasant and vice versa, beyond the first flush of young love it is in the companionship of members of their own sex that many men and women choose to spend the majority of their time. The primary help that the woman was to provide was to assist the *adam* in the task of filling the earth through child-bearing, a fact that is underlined in the later judgment upon the woman. The problem of man's aloneness is not a psychological problem of loneliness, but the fact that, without assistance, humanity's purpose cannot be achieved by the *adam* alone.

Fifth, the *adam* was created from the dust, with God breathing into him the breath of life. The woman was created with flesh and bone from the *adam*'s side while he was in a deep sleep. The woman's being derives from the man's, the man's being from the earth – the *adamah*. Adam was 'formed' while the woman is 'built'.

Sixth, the *adam* was created outside of the Garden and prior to its creation; the woman was created within it. The woman has an especial relationship to the inner world of the Garden; the *adam* has an especial relationship with the earth outside of the Garden. Also, unlike the woman, the *adam* probably witnessed God's Garden-forming activity as part of his preparation for his cultivation of the earth.

Seventh, the *adam* is given the priestly task of guarding and keeping the Garden directly by God, the woman is not. He is also given the law concerning the Tree of the Knowledge of Good and Evil, while the woman is not. It is the *adam* who will be held peculiarly responsible for the fall in the Garden. Notice also that on both of the occasions when God subsequently speaks of the law concerning the tree (3:11, 17), he addresses the *adam* in particular, speaking of it as a law both delivered to him alone and as a law concerning him most particularly and the woman only by extension. The difference between the *adam* and the woman here helps to explain how the woman could be deceived, while the man was not (the serpent plays off the information the woman had received first-hand in 1:29 against the information she had received second-hand from the *adam*).

Eighth, the *adam* is given the task of naming, as a sign and preparation for his rule over the world, while the woman is not. The *adam* also names the woman twice (first according to her nature as 'woman' in 2:23, then by her personal name 'Eve' in 3:20), while she does not name him.

Finally, in Genesis 2:24, the establishment of a marriage is described in an asymmetrical fashion, with the directionality of a man leaving his father and mother and joining his wife. I don't believe this is accidental. The bonds of human relationship and communion are chiefly formed by and in women.

Later, in the Fall of humanity, there is a breakdown of the order established by God. The *adam* fails in his task of serving and keeping the Garden and of upholding the law concerning the tree. He allows the woman to be deceived, when it was his duty to teach and protect her. The Fall was chiefly the fall of the *adam*. The woman in turn fails in her calling as helper. In the paralleled judgments that follow, both the man and the woman are told that they will experience difficult labour in the fundamental area of their activity – the man in his labour upon the ground, the woman in her labour in child-bearing – and both the man and woman will be frustrated and dominated by their source – the woman will be ruled over by the man and the man will return to the ground.

The created order is disrupted and disorder, death, and sin come into the world. However, a promise and hope of salvation is also given in the divine declaration concerning the seed of the woman and in the *adam*'s naming of the woman as the mother of all living. Sexual difference is variously disordered by the fall, but is also a means through which the disorder introduced by the fall will be overcome.

Genesis, Gender, and Sexual Difference

The difference between the sexes is a central and constitutive truth about humanity, related to our being created in the image of God. Humanity has two distinct kinds: a male kind and a female kind. Sexual dimorphism, the fact that we come in these two distinct kinds, is a fundamental fact about humanity.

Men and women are created for different primary purposes, purposes which, when pursued in unity and with mutual support, can reflect God's own form of creative rule in the world. The man's vocation, as described in Genesis 2, primarily corresponds to the tasks of the first three days of creation: to naming, taming, dividing, and ruling. The woman's vocation, by contrast, principally involves filling, glorifying, generating, establishing communion, and bringing forth new life – all tasks associated with the second three days of creation. Hence the differences between us as men and women are not merely accidental or incidental, but are integral to our purpose and deeply meaningful, relating to God's own fundamental patterns of operation. God created us to be male and female and thereby to reflect his own creative rule in his world.

The differences between men and women are related to differences between primary realms of activity and different lifeworlds. These differences are differences that will unfold and expand over time, varying from culture to culture and context to context. The root differences are expressed in unique and diverse forms from culture to culture and from individual to individual. These differences exceed any single culture and any single individual, although each individual and culture expresses and participates in them in some particular limited form.

Men and women are formed separately and differently and there is a correspondence between their nature and their purpose. The man is formed from the earth to till the ground, to serve and rule the earth. The woman is built from the man's side to bring life and communion through union. The biblical account is primarily descriptive, rather than proscriptive: men and women are created and equipped for different purposes and so will naturally exhibit different strengths, preferences, and behaviours. It should come as no surprise that the more fundamental reality of sexual dimorphism is accompanied by a vast range of secondary sexual differences, differences that typically correlate with key requirements of our primary purposes.

The different focal points of men and women's creational vocations in Genesis do not represent the full measure or scope of their callings – as if women only existed to bear children or men only to be farmers – but rather are the seeds from which broader callings can thematically develop. Each man and woman must find ways to bring the gendered aptitudes, capacities, and selves that God created them with to bear upon the situations he has placed them within. Although the centres of gravity of the sexes' callings differ, man and woman are to work together and assist each other, each employing their particular strengths to perform humanity's common task. Neither can fulfil their vocation alone.

In Genesis 1 and 2, the differences between men and women are chiefly focused upon their wider callings within the world, rather than upon their direct relationships with each other. The woman has to submit to the man's leadership, not so much because he is given direct authority over her, but because his vocation is the primary and foundational one, relating to the forming that necessarily precedes the filling in God's own creation activity. She is primarily called to fill and to glorify the structures he establishes and the world he subdues. It is less a matter of the man having authority over the woman as one of the woman following his lead. As the man forms, names, tames, establishes the foundations, and guards the boundaries, she brings life, communion, glory, and completion. Neither sex accomplishes their task alone, but must rely upon, cooperate with, and assist the other.

The differences between the sexes are also embodied differences. Possession of a womb is not something that can be detached from what it means to be a woman in Genesis, nor possession of a penis from what it means to be a man. It is not insignificant that circumcision and the opening of wombs are such central themes in the book: the conception, bearing, and raising of children are integral to the fulfilment of God's purpose. In bringing about this purpose, the man's phallic pride in his virility must be curbed by a sign of God's promise and his weakness (i.e. circumcision) and the woman's insufficiency to bear offspring must be remedied by the power of God.

Socially developed differences of gender extend out from and symbolically highlight the primary differences of our created natures and purposes. Social construction of gender is real, but it operates with the natural reality of difference between the sexes, rather than creating difference *ex nihilo* (i.e. out of nothing). The exact shape of the gendered differences between men and women vary considerably from culture to culture, yet the presence of a gender distinction between men and women is universal. Each culture has its own symbolic language of gender difference. Already within our natural bodies we see features whose purpose is not narrowly functional, but which exist for the purpose of signalling traits associated with virility or femininity to one's own or the other sex. Hair is a good example here (e.g. long hair on women, beards on men). Most cultures take these natural differences and amplify and symbolize them by means of such things as clothing. Scripture highlights the importance of such social differences in places such as 1 Corinthians 11, where Paul discusses hair, and in Deuteronomy 22:5, where women who wear men's gear and men who wear women's robes are condemned.

The rich and expansive expression of sexual difference in a vast array of culturally conjugated gender differences can be a way in which we display the *beauty* of this particular difference. The difference between men and women is more than merely a random and unstable assortment of contrasts between two classes of persons: it is the 'musical' and meaningful difference of two sexes that are inseparably related to each other. Recognising this truth, most cultures celebrate sexual difference by developing many gendered customs, forms, norms, and traditions. Rather than treating gender, as our culture is often inclined to, as a restrictive and stifling legalistic constraint, such an approach welcomes sexual difference as an often liberating manifestation of meaning and beauty that resonates with the deep reality of the creation.

In speaking of the direct relationship between man and woman, it is not difference so much as the depth and love of one flesh unity that is emphasised. Men and women are different, yet those differences are not differences designed to polarise us or pit us against each other. Rather, these differences are to be expressed in unified yet differentiated activity within the world and the closest of bonds with each other. It is not about difference from each other so much as difference for each other. What makes the woman unique is her capacity for complementing labour in profound union with the man. The animals are also helpers, but only the woman is a suitable counterpart for the *adam* in his vocation and spouse with whom he can become one flesh. The differences between men and women are precisely features that make them fitting for each other.

Healthy sexual and gender difference have been marred by the fall in various and extensive ways, through sin, bodily dysfunction, and psychological disorder. The natural processes of sexual differentiation can go awry, as Jesus discusses in the case of those 'born eunuchs' in Matthew 19:11-12. Things such as the loving one-flesh union that ought to exist between husband and wife can be shattered by divorce, or perverted by oppressive male dominance.

Concluding Reflections on Current Issues in Sexual Ethics

Within Genesis 1 and 2, we discover a foundation for reflection upon gender and sexuality more broadly, with surprising relevance to many pressing questions of sexual ethics within a contemporary context. In these concluding remarks, I want to highlight ways in which the teaching of these chapters can be brought to bear upon two key questions in contemporary sexual ethics: same-sex marriage and transgender identity.

Same-Sex Marriage

Genesis 2 in particular describes the creation of man and woman in a manner that makes clear that maleness and femaleness are not merely two illustrative instances of human diversity as such, but that together they represent a very specific and significant difference, a difference that has a peculiar importance, a difference expressly established by God at the beginning. Despite all of the variation between and within human societies, the concepts of maleness and femaleness are not ultimately formless and void of content, but relate to a reality that cuts across individuals and cultures. Genesis 2 scandalises prevailing prejudices by giving an account of the sexes that gives shape and content to their differences. It further scandalises by presenting the sexes as peculiarly and inextricably intertwined in their creation and vocation, finding their meaning and purpose in relation to each other.

Defences of same-sex relations and marriage, for instance, generally require a retreat from the scandalous specificity of the male-female relation and difference as described in Genesis 1 and 2. Yet, throughout, the specificity of the male-female relation and difference is foregrounded in these chapters. What the woman brings to the man is not companionship as such, nor mere genital relation, nor some gender neutral union. Prominent throughout Genesis 1 and 2 are the things that are peculiar to relations between men and women, things which are absent in same-sex relations. The blessing and vocation of fruitfulness is the most immediately noticeable. No same-sex union partakes of the fundamental creational blessing and calling enjoyed by the union of man and woman in marriage.

The capacity of natural marriage to traverse the most fundamental anthropological distinction – man and woman – and represent the bringing together of the two halves of humankind is another. Man and woman each peculiarly correspond to a particular aspect of God's own creative activity: men to forming and women to filling. In the union of man and woman in their distinctiveness in the fulfilment of their shared human calling we can hear some intimation of the beauty of God's own creative work in its particular form of unity and diversity.

That men and women can become 'one flesh' in marriage is a result of the fact that they are uniquely fitted for each other. The formation of the woman from the *adam*'s own flesh represents a special natural bond between the sexes that is fundamentally constitutive of each's identity: the most intimate unity of the *adam*'s own body is severed and a new person is formed out of part of himself, with whom he can enter into a new, more glorious form of unity. This form of union is only truly possible between man and woman.

the music and the meaning of male & female

The union of man and woman in marriage has an 'iconic' capacity that no other unions possess in like manner: it is not merely one of a class of intimate unions, but a unique kind of its own. This union is peculiarly connected to the image of God, reflects God's own creative labour, represents the traversal of the fundamental human difference, and the union of the two halves of humanity in the fulfilment of the fundamental human task and enjoyment of the blessing.

Each one of these facts stands against any gender neutral account of marriage. The physical dimension of marital union is not merely genital relations and excitement of erogenous zones as such, but the (re)union of two related sexes in a single 'one flesh' whole. This is a union most especially witnessed in the natural fittingness of the male-female union for the bearing of children: each sex has one half of a single sexual and reproductive system and the natural offspring of a male-female union is a positive manifestation of the 'one flesh' that bond can constitute.

Transgender Identity

Sexual difference in Genesis and the rest of Scripture is closely tied to the body and to the labour of procreation. Sexual reassignment surgery may create the appearance of the other sex's physicality, but lacks any connection to the procreative *telos* (goal) or capacity of the sexed body. It cannot be more than a hollow simulation of the reality. For this reason alone, changing one's sex can only ever be a fiction. As Oliver O'Donovan argues (in *Begotten Or Made*), holding to this fiction risks artificialising the reality of sex more generally, presenting one's sex as a matter of one's will, rather than a fact of nature to be welcomed, a form of creation ordered to a particular *telos*, rather than a matter of willed self-expression.

Oliver O'Donovan, *Begotten or Made?* (Oxford: OUP, 1984).

More generally, the body has great prominence in Christian thought. The story of the creation of man and woman is the story of the construction of bodies. The story of the gospel is largely a story of things that happened to Christ's body: conceived by the Spirit, born of the virgin, baptised by John, transfigured on the Mount, symbolically distributed at the Last Supper, crucified under Pilate, died, buried in the tomb, raised by the Spirit on the third day, caught up into heaven at the Ascension. The materiality, the objectivity, and the givenness of the body precedes and grounds our self-consciousness, activity, and self-determination. The body isn't just something that clothes the self, but is itself the self. Our bodies have been claimed by God, visibly marked out for resurrection in the rite of baptism. Our bodies must be presented to God at their root, as the limbs and organs that provide the basis for the entire superstructure of the self. We don't just have bodies that enable us to act: we are embodied selves and our bodies are the temples of the Holy Spirit. There is a unity between internal and external in the body, our interiority being inseparably connected with our exteriority, a fact often most powerfully experienced in sexual relations.

Recognising the body's existence as integral to the self should help us to recognise just how traumatic a disruption of the integrity between one's exteriority and interiority – one's alienation from one's own bodily self – could be. It is not surprising that many feel the need to address this with invasive procedures and to escape the force and reality of the disruption in social and medical pretence.

Even in their experience of a disordered sense of self, transgender persons can bear witness to the reality of sexual difference in surprising ways. Their intense alienation from their sexed bodies raises the question of why most people do not experience this and highlights the significance of the resonance between our subjectivity and the bodily objectivity of our selves, as a reality worthy of note. Their experience also pushes back against social constructivist understandings of sexed identities. If gender and sexual difference really are merely social constructs, artificial realities conjured up by society, how is it that it fails so radically in such cases? Transgender experience highlights the fact that the very self is generally experienced as gendered and that there are realms and forms of self-consciousness that we typically share with others of our sex, and which differentiate us from the other. There are also increasing scientific hints that many cases of transgender identity correlate with natural hormonal processes that have gone awry at some point in the person's development, leading to an incongruence between the person's sense of themselves as a sexed self and the sex of their body. The bodily basis of gendered subjectivities is also seen in accounts of transition, as transgender persons experience the effect of the other sex's hormones.

The body is the objectivity of the self and is the chief means by which the self is connected to and defined by others. Our bodies were not created chiefly for self-expression, but for relationship. Adam's body binds him to the earth; Eve's body binds her to Adam. The body expresses givenness – the fact that we receive ourselves from sources outside of ourselves such as our parents and ancestors, the earth, and God and that we are caught up in larger unchosen realities that precede us and produce us, such as our sex. Our bodies also express our aptitude for self-donation – our capacity to give ourselves to others. It connects us to realities that are greater than ourselves, yet which are mysteriously at work in us. Changing the sex of one's body threatens this openness of the body to the other. One's sexed body is integral to one's capacity for modes of relation: one's identity as father or mother, son or daughter, brother or sister and one's natural resonance and affinity with other members of one's sex.

By its very nature, the sexed identity that a transsexual person transitions to will always struggle to exceed a mere persona, an assumed identity that masks the reality. The transition required will also generally involve an assault upon the actual bodily self, rendering it incapable of bearing offspring, for instance, and unsuited for marriage. Given the prominent relationship between the creation of the sexes and the calling and blessing of procreation in Genesis, this is a serious thing indeed.

Scripture clearly and unequivocally punctures the fictions at the heart of much contemporary transgender ideology. However, we must distinguish clearly between transgender *ideology* and transgender *persons*. There are transgender persons who recognise the integrity and importance of sexual difference, deny the possibility of actually becoming a member of the other sex, yet argue for the tragic necessity of extreme measures to manage what they understand as their disorders of gendered subjectivity. I believe that a far deeper sensitivity and caution than many conservative Christians have typically shown in relation to transgender persons is required in such cases.

Scripture firmly closes the doors to the option of transition and defines sex and the gendered self in a manner that makes transition from one sex to another impossible. However, Scripture's recognition of exceptions to the regular norms of sexual difference (those 'born eunuchs' in Matthew 19, who are most likely intersex persons) and its provision of means of relief in cases of irresolvable brokenness such as divorce – means of relief that are tragic testimonies to the work of sin and death – does, I believe, leave us with difficult questions of what to do in certain exceptional or extreme cases. For instance, what do we do with XY intersex persons with complete androgen insensitivity syndrome (CAIS), who are chromosomally and gonadally male, yet apparently female in external genitalia and gender identity? What do we do in the case of the person whose gender dysphoria has led them to attempt suicide and for whom some form of identification with the other sex is the only realistic option that they or the professionals helping them can envisage for addressing their problems?

When dealing with such exceptions or extreme cases, considerable prudence and patience may be required, as the norms may not readily or straightforwardly apply (although they are invariably relevant for the process of our deliberation) and certain accommodations may need to be made for a brokenness that cannot be overcome. In dealing with transgender persons, we may face similar questions to those we experience when dealing with the messy relationships that exist in a society where the institution of marriage is unravelling. Is an appropriate emphasis and insistence upon biblical ideals something that leaves us unable to deal well with people in intractably compromised or complicated realities?

I don't believe that it is. In fact, a clear understanding of the biblical norms is a prerequisite for understanding and speaking to such realities. Wisely and compassionately recognising and handling such complicated, exceptional, or extreme cases, while maintaining the clarity and authority of the scriptural norms, and resisting unbiblical compromise, is the challenge we face.

Here it is important that we always keep in mind both Genesis 1-2 and Genesis 3: there is a good natural order to the world created by God and a disruption of that order by sin and death. We must never allow recognition of the disruption of the natural order to represent a denial of its continuing force and goodness and of our duty to uphold and pursue it. In upholding the goodness of the natural order, however, we must acknowledge that this order has been unsettled, occasionally in ways that cannot be rectified or overcome in this life. For instance, there are tragic cases where the natural distinction between male and female is unclear.

In dealing with matters such as transgender identity or same-sex marriage, it is important to bring into focus the temporal context in which the scriptural teaching regarding the body, the sexes, and marriage is developed. Marriage and the body are not unchanging realities. Rather, marriage is a calling peculiarly pertaining to this present age, in which the world must be subdued and filled. Once the new creation is ushered in, whatever place marriage still has, it will definitely be a radically transformed one, and will be characterised more by fulfilment than by ongoing vocation. It will also be eclipsed by the greater realities of Christ and his bride to which it points and in which, in some measure, we already participate.

Likewise, although our bodies are currently afflicted by sin, alienation, and death, and manifest the unravelling of the natural order, they await a great 'transition'. Transgender persons, who can experience the post-Fall alienation of the body in an especially acute form, are not to be faulted in longing for a transition, although the particular 'transitions' that they obtain will not effect the redemption of the body that we all need. Part of the witness of the Church in such situations must be a recovery of the centrality of the body as the temple of the Holy Spirit, the limbs and organs of Christ, the object of divine redemption, and site of salvation. In baptism, as I have already noted, there is a powerful witness to the temporality of our bodies: our Fall-scarred bodies are marked out by the reality of Christ's death and visibly set apart for future resurrection. There are wrongs that cannot be righted now, brokenness that cannot be repaired, wounds that cannot be healed. Yet in such declarations of divine promise, powerfully directed to our very bodies themselves, and in the Church's communion of the Spirit that they manifest and produce, we can find hope and strength to endure. There is coming a time when all tears will be wiped away, every injustice rectified, everything lost restored, and the weakness and mortality of our earthly bodies overwhelmed in a life that will well up eternal. P

the music and the meaning of male & female

NO LONGER TABOO

Reflections and resources on the homosexuality debate
Sam Allberry

It is hard to believe that just a little more than a decade ago it was very rare to find a Christian book on homosexuality. The issue was not absent, of course, but it was very little discussed. Well the world has changed dramatically since then, and the Christian world has been impacted hugely too, with mixed results.

On the plus side, there is now much more of a readiness to discuss homosexuality in our churches. The issue is no longer taboo. It is much easier now for Christians to be open about struggles with temptation in this area. Churches are more ready to teach into it and to offer good pastoral counsel.

But with the explosion of attention on issues of sexuality has also come enormous confusion. Even in churches with a good heritage of biblical teaching many of our members are not clear about what the Bible says about homosexuality, or even if such clarity is possible. Others might be very certain about the biblical prohibitions in this area but utterly unsure how to be an encouragement or blessing to a fellow-believer struggling with same-sex temptation, or how to be a friend to a non-Christian neighbour from the LGBT community. We clearly have a lot more to learn and to teach.

Thankfully there is now extensive literature to help. We must give thanks for our evangelical publishing houses who have been willing to publish faithful materials on an issue that can elicit a huge amount of hostility. It may seem as though our bookcases are now heaving with good books on this issue, but it wasn't always so.

What follows is an informal survey of some of the literature that is out there, and which pastors in particular need to be aware of.

1. LITERATURE FROM A REVISIONIST VIEWPOINT

The most popular work arguing for same-sex relationships is *God and the Gay Christian* by Matthew Vines. Vines first came to prominence as a result of a YouTube video he produced outlining why he believed the Bible allowed for same-sex relationships. Vines is young, bright and evangelical, and the video quickly went viral. The book sets out his position more fully. The power of Vines' book isn't so much that he's breaking new ground. By his own admission, he is drawing heavily upon, and popularising, the work of others, most notably James Brownson. No, the power of Vines' work is how forcefully he makes his case. His book remains the most compelling for the revisionist position.

Matthew Vines, *God and the Gay Christian: The Biblical Case in Support of Same-Sex Relationships* (New York: Convergent, 2014).

You can still access the video on YouTube, searching for *"The Gay Debate: The Bible and Homosexuality."*

James V. Brownson, *Bible, Gender, Sexuality: Reframing the Church's Debate on Same-Sex Relationships* (Grand Rapids: Eerdmans, 2013).

Vines' starting point is what he describes as the "bad fruit" of the traditional orthodox position on human sexuality. He shares heart-wrenching stories of young gay people excluded and hurt by their Christian communities. The book packs a hefty emotional punch. And herein lies its biggest danger and weakness. It is dangerous because stories like this leave us reeling, and desperate for the Bible to say something more affirming on this issue. It is the book's weakness, because it is, in essence, an emotional argument seeking exegetical justification. Vines takes us through the main texts on homosexuality to set about proving that our traditional reading of them misunderstands them.

Vines writes accessibly and winsomely. This is the book many of us in church ministry need to reckon with. Because the power of the book lies in the emotional narrative that drives it, we need to be able to demonstrate not only that his exegetical arguments are weak (that has been done easily enough) but, far more importantly, that the Bible gives us far better narratives than the world. Critique of his arguments is not enough. We need to respond to narrative with narrative. (This is why a number of us have worked so hard on the website *LivingOut.org* – we need to show that the church has her own, better stories to tell on human sexuality.)

The weakest point in Vines' argument (and in most of the revisionist cases I've seen) is the failure to come to terms with the very clear way in which Scripture ties the institution of marriage to our sexual difference as men and women. It is not, ultimately, what Paul says about homosexuality that is determinative (though what he says is both very clear and significant), but what Jesus says about marriage. We do not have a doctrine of homosexuality, but a doctrine of marriage, and what we believe about sexuality and sexual ethics flows from this. The key texts, therefore are Genesis 1-2 and Jesus' use of them in Matthew 19:3ff. These are the passages revisionists tend to skip over. Arguing about what Paul did and didn't mean in Romans 1 or 1 Corinthians 6 ends up being a bit of a smokescreen.

> WE DO NOT HAVE A DOCTRINE OF HOMOSEXUALITY, BUT A DOCTRINE OF MARRIAGE, AND WHAT WE BELIEVE ABOUT SEXUALITY AND SEXUAL ETHICS FLOWS FROM THIS.

2. Literature from a Conservative Viewpoint

There are a number of very helpful books supporting an orthodox, traditional position on homosexuality.

In *The Secret Thoughts of an Unlikely Convert*, Rosaria Butterfield provides an account of her conversion from a lesbian lifestyle (she was Professor of English and Queer Theory at Syracuse University) to conservative Christianity (she is now the wife of a Presbyterian pastor, and full-time homeschools their adopted children). It is heart-warming and powerful. A key lesson from Rosaria's story is the role Christian hospitality played in her conversion to Christ. Many members of our churches may feel ill-equipped to reach out to LGBT friends and neighbours, but Rosaria's testimony shows the power of normal Christian friendship and hospitality.

Rosaria Champagne Butterfield, *The Secret Thoughts of an Unlikely Convert* (Pittsburgh: Crown & Covenant, 2012).

Her recent follow-up book, *Openness Unhindered*, continues the story and adds some deeper reflections on how we think as Christians about homosexuality. Her material on the ways in which sexual desires are categorised into fixed 'orientations' is particularly urgent. Both books are written beautifully (you can tell this is someone who has spent decades around literature) and are accessible to the general reader.

Rosaria Champagne Butterfield, *Openness Unhindered: Further Thoughts of an Unlikely Convert on Sexual Identity and Union with Christ* (Pittsburgh: Crown & Covenant, 2015).

There are some excellent books going through the biblical teaching on sex and sexuality. The most thorough is Robert Gagnon's *The Bible and Homosexual Practice*. This is not a book for the faint-hearted. It is 520 pages and is highly technical. But his conclusions are utterly compelling. It is telling how many revisionists avoid interacting with his scholarship altogether. This will not be a book for the general church membership, but is a must-read for pastors and those in leadership.

Robert A J Gagnon, *The Bible and Homosexual Practice: Texts and Hermeneutics* (Nashville: Abingdon Press, 2002).

Kevin DeYoung, *What Does the Bible Really Teach About Homosexuality?* (Nottingham: IVP, 2015).

Gagnon's was one of the first books I read on the Bible and homosexuality, and I remember thinking afterwards how much we needed something that tackled the same passages, drawing on the same depth of scholarship, but written at a popular level. In my mind, it needed to be written by a pastor-scholar – someone like Kevin de Young. So it was a thrill to discover de Young was actually working on such a book. *What does the Bible Really Teach About Homosexuality?* is one of the best books on this topic out there. De Young covers the key biblical texts, those dealing with homosexuality explicitly as well as those which are foundational for our understanding of marriage. He looks at some of the ways in which revisionists have handled these texts and demonstrates ably how these passages do speak with clarity and consistency and reinforce the teaching of the whole Bible that any sexual activity outside of heterosexual marriage is forbidden by God. As well as dealing with these passages, de Young also spends time answering some of the common objections to the traditional Christian position on homosexuality, such as concerns about being on the "wrong side of history" or that the biblical authors only knew of a very different kind of homosexuality to the committed partnerships we are seeing in society today. Dealing with these objections as well as the key passages makes this an essential handbook for the pastor and church member alike. It is top of my list of books to recommend.

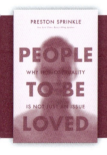

Preston Sprinkle, *People to Be Loved: Why Homosexuality Is Not Just an Issue* (Grand Rapids: Zondervan, 2015).

Coming from a similar viewpoint (mostly) is Preston Sprinkle's book, *People To Be Loved: Why Homosexuality Is Not Just An Issue*. Sprinkle is writing for the sceptic and this is reflected in his tone. He is gentle and gracious throughout. He handles the biblical passages very well (though I disagree with his conclusion that Sodom and Gomorrah is not instructive about God's attitude to homosexuality). It is a great book to give to someone who is hostile to the traditional Christian position but willing to look at the issue. As such, it is good for those who are in, or leaning toward, the Matthew Vines camp. The main flaw in the book, baffling given Sprinkle's careful handling of the relevant scriptural passages, is that he concludes this is not a gospel issue. On that he is, I think, seriously mistaken. Paul, after all, makes it very clear in 1 Cor 6:9-10 that this is a salvation issue: those who do not repent of this lifestyle will not enter God's kingdom. Similarly, Jesus rebukes the church in Thyatira for its tolerance of teaching that leads believers into sexual sin (see Rev 2:20). He does not just rebuke those responsible for such teaching, but the wider church community that tolerates the presence of it.

Taking a slightly different approach is *Do Ask, Do Tell, Let's Talk: Why and How Christians Should Have Gay Friends* by Brad Hambrick. Hambrick's aim (as the title suggests) is to equip and motivate Christians to be reaching out in friendship to those in the gay community. That being the case, the book does not treat what the Bible says about homosexuality; that is not his priority (though he is writing from a conservative viewpoint). It is not designed to be the first book a Christian reads on the topic, but would be a great book to read *after* that. Hambrick provides really helpful material on how we can forge genuine and meaningful friendships, and the book is full of practical insights and suggestions. I would recommend it highly to those who are already biblically convinced about what the Bible says, but who wouldn't instinctively know how to be, say, a good neighbour to a gay couple. If we're tempted to think the last thing we need is a book telling us how to make friends, I suspect we are precisely the people who most need to read this.

Brad Hambrick, *Do Ask, Do Tell, Let's Talk: Why and How Christians Should Have Gay Friends* (Minneapolis: Cruciform Press, 2016).

A book on how the whole church can respond healthily to the issue of homosexuality is Ed Shaw's *The Plausibility Problem*. Shaw doesn't so much zero in on homosexuality itself but on the various missteps the church has taken on related issues which account for why it is floundering so much now. Shaw tackles matters such as the idolatry of marriage, the ways in which we make the biological family – and not the wider spiritual family – the basic unit of church life, and the general downplaying of sacrifice in the Christian life. All these trends have made it much harder for Christians to believe in the plausibility of the Bible's stance on homosexuality, especially the life of celibacy many will need to face. Given the book ranges around these related issues, it applies far more widely than to the issue of sexuality. It is a wonderful book to read for creating a healthy church culture generally. If your church is full of lonely people and others are finding it hard to find a sense of family among God's people, it is vital reading.

Ed Shaw, *The Plausibility Problem* (Nottingham: IVP, 2015).

I should probably say something about my own book, *Is God Anti-Gay?* This is very short (under a hundred pages) and structured around the most common questions asked about same-sex attraction. I hope it serves as a first port of call, introducing people to the basic biblical lie of the land and some of the issues that come up in these discussions so that their appetites are whetted for more in-depth reading and study.

Sam Allberry, *Is God Anti-Gay?* (Epsom: The Good Book Company, 2013).

no longer taboo

3. ISSUES OF ONGOING SIGNIFICANCE

Is same-sex attraction itself sinful?

This is a matter of ongoing contention. It sounds like it should require a simple yes/no answer, but it is actually a little trickier than that, and pastorally quite a fraught issue to talk about.

Co-authors Denny Burk and Heath Lambert address it in their book *Transforming Homosexuality: What the Bible Says about Sexual Orientation and Change* (Phillipsburg, New Jersey: P & R Publishing, 2015), arguing that it is sinful; Wesley Hill in both his books *Washed and Waiting* and *Spiritual Friendship* argues that it is not, and that same-sex attraction is "redeemable." Wesley Hill, *Washed and Waiting: Reflections on Christian Faithfulness and Homosexuality* (Grand Rapids: Zondervan, 2010); Wesley Hill, *Spiritual Friendship: Finding Love in the Church as a Celibate Gay Christian* (Grand Rapids: Brazos, 2015). The debate also featured in the form of a discussion featuring Burk, Hill and Preston Sprinkle at the annual meeting of the Evangelical Theological Society in 2014. The discussion between them has continued online via their respective blogs and websites.

A significant part of the problem is that different people mean different things by "same-sex attraction." For some, it refers to the specific and sinful desires themselves: same-sex sexual attraction and unhealthy emotional dependency. If this is what it means, then clearly these are not right. Sinful desires are sinful.

So far so good. But what about temptation to these things? Does that count as sin? We know that indulging sinful desires mentally is sinful along with indulging them physically. Jesus warns us that lustful looks, as well as lustful acts, are sinful. So while it is common to speak of a distinction between experiencing same-sex desires and engaging in homosexual activity, we must be careful not to suggest that whatever is going on in our head, provided it remains in our head, is okay up until the point we physically act on it. Indulging sexual fantasies in our head is a form of sexual sin.

But Christians have long kept a distinction between temptation and sin. We see this reflected in Scripture. In the Lord's Prayer Jesus teaches us to pray for forgiveness for sin but deliverance from temptation. The two are not the same. James – Jesus' younger half-brother – writes that temptation gives birth to sin. They may be on the same continuum, but are different stages on it. The Christian fighting temptation is not sinning. The experience of temptation is not sin; it is what we do with it that is significant on that point.

But this is not to suggest that our temptations are utterly alien to us or that we are just passive victims of them. James also tells us that temptations come from our own hearts. We do need to take ownership of that. When I am tempted it is right that I acknowledge the way in which the very fact I am being tempted is a reflection of how my desires have been disordered by the fall. (This is one way in which our temptations differ from those experienced by Jesus. Ours have an internal source; his did not.)

Those who push the "same-sex attraction is sin" line, I suspect, are trying to argue against those who posit our sexual desires as being neutral. They are not neutral. They are a consequence of the fall. We wouldn't experience them if we weren't sinners. But experiencing them is not, in and of itself, an act of sin, provided we are fleeing from such temptation and pursuing Christ. God does not promise that our temptations will completely disappear in this life. But he does promise to help us stand up under them. We have a duty to do so.

But there are other people who use the language of "same-sex attraction" in a much broader sense. For them, it is not just a matter of the sinful same-sex desires we experience, but of all the other things that often seem to be experienced alongside them: an unusual capacity and longing for deep friendship with people of the same sex, a greater emotional intelligence and sensitivity, and some other traits that might not fit the typical cultural view of masculinity. If these things are all part of the package, then the phrase "same-sex attraction is sin" is heard as being "who you are, even when you're not really doing anything, is an act of sin." Clearly we need to be very clear about what we do and don't mean by the terms we use. Some of the things described above are morally neutral or good. Whether it is appropriate to link them in with "same-sex attraction" is a discussion we need to have. Clearly in a number of cases they are experienced together.

It is not uncommon for younger Christians when coming to terms with the presence of same-sex attraction to feel especially dirty and crushed by the experience, even when such desires are both unwelcome and resisted. A young believer, feeling himself to be beyond the pale, needs at that point to hear the tenderness of the one who does not break a bruised reed. An unqualified "same-sex attraction is sin" comment can be pastorally devastating. It may be literally true, but without further explanation or qualification, can be as useful as the counsel proffered by Job's companions.

Connecting homosexuality to biblical theology

I suspect that part of the reason many Christians have struggled to articulate or maintain a faithful response to the issue of homosexuality is that we have separated this issue from the wider themes of the Bible. Homosexuality is not mentioned much in the Bible. It is not close to being what the Bible is about. But it does flow from what is a central theme in Scripture, and which takes us to the very heart of the gospel itself. What Scripture says about *marriage* introduces us to be the narrative of the whole Bible.

The Bible begins with the marriage of Adam and Eve in the Garden of Eden and ends with the marriage of the Lamb and his bride. The first is the trailer for the second, a pointer to it and earthly reflection of it. The coming together of male and female in the first chapter of the Bible is the anticipation of the coming together of heaven and earth in the final chapter. Marriage is a picture of the thing God is doing in the universe, drawing together a people for his Son, Jesus Christ. It is this narrative that undergirds all reality and shapes our view of marriage. Marriage is not, for the Christian, merely a public recognition and celebration of two people's deep feelings for one another. It is a covenant by which two unlike parties are joined together for life. It is why we insist on couple's saying "I will" rather than "I do." What concerns us is not the couple's feelings for one another in the present moment (as if those feelings weren't already obvious enough), but their intentions for the future. It is also why we understand marriage to be necessarily heterosexual. It is the union of like and unlike, of male and female, precisely because it pictures the union of Christ and his church. A man and a man, or a woman and a woman, cannot picture this deep reality.

Marriage reflects the gospel, and because of this we cannot change our view of marriage without ultimately changing our view of the gospel. Matthew 19 is the most significant chapter in the Bible on homosexuality even though it doesn't mention homosexuality, because it is one of the clearest passages on marriage. What we

MARRIAGE REFLECTS
BECAUSE OF THIS WE
VIEW OF MARRIAGE
CHANGING OUR VIEW

believe about homosexuality flows from what we believe about marriage.

Recovering this perspective, I think, helps us enormously to respond in a healthy way to homosexuality. It reminds us that there is a rationale behind the sexual ethics presented consistently throughout the whole Bible. God's prohibitions against spiritual intermarriage, sex outside of marriage, and against same-sex unions all make sense given the unique role marriage has in reflecting the union of Christ and his people. It is not that God is arbitrarily against certain forms of sex for no apparent reason. The insistence in both Old and New Testaments that sex is for marriage between one man and one woman fits perfectly into this biblical-theological context.

It also helps us deal with some of the significant apologetic challenges that arise when homosexuality is discussed. If our explanation of why the Bible does not affirm homosexual relationships centres on God's plan for marriage reflecting what he is doing in the world through Christ, then we are moving the discussion towards the very heart of the gospel. We need not fear this issue arising and becoming a distraction from the gospel. We can begin to formulate an apologetic that sets questions about homosexuality in the wider context of the one who has come as the perfect groom to win a people for himself. **p**

THE GOSPEL, AND CANNOT CHANGE OUR WITHOUT ULTIMATELY OF THE GOSPEL.

COMPASSION WITHOUT COMPROMISE

Robert S. Smith gives a pastoral response to the transgender crisis.

The issue of transgenderism is both confusing and controversial. The *confusion* is over what is real and what is moral. The reality question boils down to this: Is it the case that a person can be born with "the wrong body" or are they simply confused in their psychology? The morality question has many faces. For example, should a person be allowed to use the bathroom that corresponds to their subjective gender identity? Or should children with gender identity issues be given puberty blockers?

The source of the *controversy* does not simply lie in the different ways these questions are answered but in the different worldviews that lie beneath the surface. One claims that a person's gender should be based on the objective fact of their biological sex. Where there is a perceived 'mismatch', then subjectivity should yield to objectivity. The other claims that the objective facts of biology are irrelevant to gender identity. In fact, all objectivity must give way to a person's own subjective gender perception.

In light of such a worldview divide, and the far-reaching changes being wrought by the acceptance of transgender ideology, Christians need to search the Scriptures carefully and prayerfully to see how God would have us respond. The main purpose of this essay is to begin such a search and to outline the shape of a biblically informed pastoral response. However, before we do, it will help us to clarify a number of key terms and probe a little further into transgender ideology.

1. KEY TERMS AND THEIR MEANINGS

Biological sex or birth sex: These terms refer to whether one is male or female on the basis of anatomical characteristics such as internal and external sexual organs, chromosomes, hormones, and secondary sex characteristics – e.g. body shape, voice pitch and hair distribution. Biological sex is often simply referred to as "sex."

Gender identity: This refers to the way individuals perceive themselves and wish to name themselves. When a person's subjective gender identity conforms to their objective biological sex, which is the case for most people, they may be referred to cisgender (cis = on this side of). When there is a clash, however, then they are commonly referred to as transgender (trans = on the other side of).

Gender expression: This refers to the psychological and social aspects of how masculinity and femininity are presented in things like dress and demeanour, social roles and conventions and other cultural gender norms. These vary from culture to culture, if not person to person. It is worth noting that the distinction between sex and gender is not universal and in ordinary speech they are often used interchangeably.

Gender roles: This refers to the commonly-accepted expectations of maleness or femaleness, including social and behavioural expectations. Whilst some roles (e.g. who cooks the meals) change from person to person, household to household or culture to culture, others are biologically determined (e.g. pregnancy and breastfeeding).

Gender bending: This refers to the intentional crossing or bending or blending of accepted gender roles, perhaps by adopting the dress, mannerisms or behaviours of the alternate binary gender, or through the attempt to obscure one's gender and to appear as either asexual or androgynous.

Gender dysphoria: This is the diagnostic term for the distress experienced by those whose psychological or emotional gender identity differs from their biological or birth sex.

Intersex: This is a general term that covers a range of disorders of sexual development (DSDs) where there is some biological ambiguity in a person's genitalia or gonads, or more rarely still, their chromosomes. Except in very rare instances, a person's biological sex can be known from their DNA. Because intersex conditions are medically identifiable deviations from the sexual binary norm they are not regarded as constituting a third sex, and many intersex people do not wish to be part of the LGBTQ movement.

Transgender: This is an umbrella term for people who are born either male or female, but whose gender identity differs from their birth sex (to varying degrees), and who want to express the gender with which they identify through cross-dressing, and/or cross-hormone therapy, and/ or sex reassignment surgery. The term transsexual is sometimes used interchangeably with transgender, and sometimes used only of those who seek medical assistance to transition.

Heteronormativity: This is the view that biological sex is either male or female, that sex and gender are meant to go together, and that only sexual orientation toward and sexual relations with a member of the opposite sex is normal and natural. As we will see, heteronormativity is essentially the biblical view of sex and gender, but it is increasing regarded as oppressive, homophobic and transphobic.

2. THE BRAVE NEW WORLD OF GENDER PLASTICITY

2.1. A question of identity

The question – "Who am I?" – is by no means new. Nevertheless, it is being asked today with a new force and in a new form. The old form assumes there is an objective 'I' that already exists and is waiting to be discovered. The new form denies this assumption and so asks a different question – *"What do I identify as?"* – which speaks of chosenness (rather than givenness), of changeability (rather than fixity).

This highlights two notions that lie at the heart of this new worldview: 'gender diversity' and 'gender fluidity.' Gender diversity asserts that gender is not a binary reality, but exists on a broad spectrum. Gender fluidity asserts that people can move back and forth along that spectrum.

However, not all are quite so ready to embrace the prospect of perpetual fluidity, nor to dispense with sexual binarism. In fact, many of those who identify as transgender have a very strong sense of the gender binary (not gender diversity). Similarly, many of those who experience gender dysphoria are not seeking gender fluidity, but want their body to be (or appear to be) that of the other sex. This is one of many tensions within the LGBTQ movement.

Nevertheless, the slender but common thread that seeks to hold the LGBTQ movement together is the idea that subjective feelings of identity trump objective facts of biology. Where, then, did such an idea come from? And how has it come upon us so suddenly?

2.2. The transgender 'tipping point'

It is generally agreed that a transgender 'tipping point' was reached in western society sometime in 2013. Sociologically speaking, a 'tipping point' refers to that moment in time when a minority is able to change the thinking and/or behaviour of the majority – a change that presupposes the weakening, if not the reversal, of long-held attitudes and practices. Evidence that such a dramatic change has taken place is all around us.

But, despite the appearance of 'suddenness', the change has, in fact, been happening incrementally for the last half a century. Ever since the late 1960s, transgender theorists have been seeking to sever the connection between gender and sex. Sex is still seen as an objective *biological* reality, but not as determinative of gender. Gender is determined either by one's own choice (in what's known as the voluntarist stream of transgender ideology) or by psychosocial forces (in the constructivist stream) or by independent neurological factors (in the determinist stream) or by some combination of these (and perhaps other) factors. Either way, there is no necessary connection between a person's biological sex and their gender identity.

2.3. Queer theory and queer theology

However, some want to take things even further. For example, the ultimate goal of many queer theorists who have been driving forces behind the LGBTQ movement is not only to eliminate 'heteronormativity' and banish binary categories, but to reject every kind of label. As one advocate puts it: "At the heart of Queer culture is revolution. The truest rebellion against a world built on categories, labels and binaries is coming from the emergence of identities that refuse to conform."

Lily Edelstein, "Sexual fluidity: Living a label-free life." *ABC News* (20 Feb, 2016).

Similar sentiments are echoed by queer theologians, like former evangelical, Virginia Ramey Mollenkott: "All of us are therefore called to confront the binary gender construct for our own good and the good of those who are transgender. Because gender roles are by no means equitable, binary gender assumptions and roles are devastating to all of us – 'masculine' men, 'feminine' women, and those somewhere in the middle."

> Virginia Ramey Mollenkott, "Gender Diversity and Christian Community." *The Other Side*, May-June 2001, Vol. 37, No. 3.

Mollenkott therefore champions an omnigender future in which everyone "would have their own unique sexuality, falling in love with another person because of their emotional response to the person's entire being, not the person's genitals." In such a future, government documents would not record a person's sex or gender, individuals would be free to change their bodies by any means available, and all bathrooms, sports and even prisons would be unisex. Those who fear such a prospect, Mollenkott claims, are reacting "out of loyalty to the idea that there really is an essential feminine and masculine binary that is either God's will or nature's perpetual norm or both."

> Virginia Ramey Mollenkott, *Omnigender: A Trans-Religious Approach* (Cleveland: Pilgrim Press, 2007), 167.
>
> Ibid., 8.

2.4. How should Christians respond?

How, then, should Christians respond to such a challenge? Our first and fundamental responsibility is to live by every word that comes from God's mouth. This means we must listen carefully to what the Bible teaches us about human sexuality and gender identity, and then work out how we are to live, love and minister in a very confused culture, and to the many confused individuals within it.

This, in turn, means that we have both a pastoral task and a political task. As the primary concern of this essay is the former, it will help to identify some of the key pastoral questions as we turn to examine the Scriptures:

- *How do we teach and encourage those who are conflicted and confused by the social changes going on around us?*
- *How do we counsel and care for those who, through no apparent fault of their own, experience a profound sense of gender dysphoria?*
- *How do we effectively evangelise gender non-conforming people?*
- *What does repentance mean for someone who has undergone gender transition?*
- *What does Christian discipleship look like for someone who battles ongoing gender dysphoria?*

3. BIBLICAL AND THEOLOGICAL CONSIDERATIONS

3.1. The binary nature of biological sex and its relationship to gender

The basic, binary and sexually dimorphic nature of humanity is clearly established in Genesis 1:

> *Gen 1:26-27*
>
> Then God said, "Let us make mankind in our image…"
> So God created mankind in his own image,
> in the image of God he created him;
> male and female he created them.

The implication of the text is clear: there is no third sex. Lest we be in any doubt, this is underlined by none other than Jesus himself:

> *Matt 19:4*
> *cf. Mark 10:6*
>
> "Haven't you read," he replied [to the Pharisees], "that at the beginning the Creator 'made them male and female'…?"

The binary reality of human sexuality revealed in Genesis 1 is further emphasised and developed in Genesis 2:

> *Gen 2:24-25*
>
> That is why a man leaves his father and mother and is united to his wife, and they become one flesh. Adam and his wife were both naked, and they felt no shame.

The clear implication of this is that *biological sex determines both gender identity and gender roles*. That is, human males grow into men (and potentially husbands and fathers) and human females grow into women (and potentially wives and mothers). Indeed such heteronormativity makes both human marriage and human family possible. Jesus again confirms this, bringing Genesis 1 and 2 into the closest possible connection:

> *Mark 10:6-8*
>
> "But at the beginning of creation God 'made them male and female'. 'For this reason a man will leave his father and mother and be united to his wife, and the two will become one flesh.'"

The implication is once again clear: men and women are not two poles at either end of a gender spectrum. Indeed, as we'll see, there is no space in the biblical worldview – either pre or post-fall – for a third gender.

3.2. The impact of the fall

That is not to say that human sexuality and gender identity are always straightforward. Indeed, the Bible has plenty to say about the effects of the fall on every aspect of our humanity, including our sexuality and gender identity. Because sin is in the world and the whole created order has been subjected to frustration, things go wrong – both psychologically (with our minds) and physiologically (with our bodies).

One of the ways the Bible acknowledges this latter fact is by introducing us to the category of the eunuch. In fact, in Matthew 19, following his discussion of marriage and the grounds for divorce and remarriage, Jesus distinguishes between three types of eunuchs: two literal and one metaphorical or spiritual.

> *For there are eunuchs who were born that way, and there are eunuchs who have been made eunuchs by others – and there are those who choose to live like eunuchs for the sake of the kingdom of heaven. The one who can accept this should accept it.*
>
> Matt 19:12

The first of these categories – eunuchs from birth – almost certainly would have included the numerous conditions that today fall under the 'intersex' umbrella. However, the Scriptures do not present eunuchs as a 'third gender.' In fact, every eunuch we meet in Scripture is presented as male – albeit a male who is (presumably) unable to function sexually or procreatively (Isa 56:3), either due to a birth defect or human intervention. In other words, the Scriptures resist diluting the sex/gender binary, even though some do not fit neatly into it. Those tragic exceptions are a post-fall phenomenon and, consequently, are best seen as "medically identifiable deviations from the human binary sexual norm."

Contrary to the suggestion of Megan K. de Franza, *Sex Difference in Christian Theology: Male, Female, and Intersex in the Image of God* (Grand Rapids: Eerdmans, 2015), 66.

Interestingly, the Intersex Society of North America is opposed to the idea that intersex people constitute a third gender on pragmatic grounds. See: www.isna.org/faq/third-gender

"Gender Identity Harms Children," American College of Pediatricians, August, 2016, online: www.acpeds.org/the-college-speaks/position-statements/gender-dysphoria-in-children

3.3. Prohibitions against gender bending

If there are tragic afflictions that flow from the fall, Scripture also alerts to ways in which humanity instinctively rebels against God's design. This is clear from the Bible's condemnation of a variety of 'gender bending' behaviours.

(i) The first of these is cross-dressing.

> *A woman must not wear men's clothing, nor a man wear women's clothing, for the Lord your God detests anyone who does this.*
>
> Deut 22:5

That this text condemns cross-dressing in the strongest possible terms is clear from the use of the term 'abomination' (that is, something detestable, repulsive or loathsome), which is applied to any act that is "excluded by its very nature" or is "dangerous or sinister." The same Hebrew word is applied to homosexual intercourse (Lev 18:22; 20:13) and various idolatrous practices (Deut 7:5; 13:14).

> Ernst Jenni and Claus Westermann, *Theological Lexicon of the Old Testament* (Peabody: Hendrickson, 1997), 1429.

But why should cross-dressing be seen in such terms? Many commentators have assumed a link with either homosexuality or pagan religion. However, there is nothing in the immediate context that suggests this. Rather, as Daniel Block concludes, "this injunction seeks to preserve the order built into creation, specifically the fundamental distinction between male and female. For a person to wear anything associated with the opposite gender confuses one's sexual identity and blurs established boundaries."

> Daniel I. Block, *The NIV Application Commentary: Deuteronomy* (Grand Rapids: Zondervan, 2012), 512.

(ii) The second is sexual effeminacy; that is, a man playing the part of a woman (by being the 'receiver') in homosexual intercourse. In 1 Cor 6:9 Paul lists those who will not inherit the kingdom of God if they persist in their activities and he includes among them "men who have sex with men." As the NIV footnote says, "behind that phrase lie two terms that refer to the passive and active participants in homosexual acts." Those terms are *malakoi* and *arsenokoitai* respectively. What's significant for us is the way in which Paul condemns the *malakoi*, along with the *arsenokoitai*. As Robert Gagnon argues, part of Paul's concern about the behaviour of the *malakoi* is most likely that it represents the feminisation of those men. While it is true that "the first and most heinous stage of feminization occurred in the act of sexual penetration: being lain with 'as though a woman,'" it is also likely that for Paul the most troubling examples of the *malakoi* were "those who engage in a process of feminization to erase further their masculine appearance and manner."

> Robert J. Gagnon, *The Bible and Homosexual Practice* (Nashville: Abingdon Press, 2002), 311.

> Ibid., 312.

(iii) The third of the behaviours that the Bible opposes is gender ambiguity; that is, trying to blur the lines between male and female.

1 Cor 11:13-15 | *Judge for yourselves: is it proper for a woman to pray to God with her head uncovered? Does not the very nature of things teach you that if a man has long hair, it is a disgrace to him, but that if a woman has long hair, it is her glory? For long hair is given to her as a covering.*

Whilst there are a number of obscurities in the passage in which these verses appear, what is clear is that Paul desires men and women to both maintain and celebrate the gender distinctions with which we have been created, rather than deny or diminish them.

compassion without compromise

(iv) As we reflect on the implications of the Bible's teaching, it is important to recognise that none of these passages suggest that those with genuine gender dysphoria are necessarily culpable for their condition. Unlike wilful, rebellious gender bending or gender erasing (which are certainly prohibited by such texts), the experience of gender dysphoria would appear to be a largely non-volitional (and so non-moral) affliction. Consequently, our first response to those who suffer from it ought to be compassion, not condemnation.

However, the Bible's teaching certainly has implications for how sufferers try to manage their dysphoria. There are right and wrong ways to address or manage all of life's challenges, including mental health issues like gender incongruence. It therefore needs to be said that, from a biblical point of view, trying to obliterate, disguise or live at odds with one's God-given gender is contrary to both God's will and the sufferer's good.

3.4. The saving and sanctifying power of Jesus

What, then, is the way forward?

(i) The first thing to appreciate is that all who confess Jesus as Lord and believe in their hearts that God raised him from the dead are justified from sin, brought to new birth and given a new identity as sons and daughters of God. "Therefore," writes Paul, "if anyone is in Christ, the new creation has come: the old has gone, the new is here!" (2 Cor 5:17). This vital, spiritual union is necessarily determinative of a whole new self-understanding (Gal 2:20a). In short, no Christian is what they once were (1 Cor 6:11), for Christ has taken from us all that defiled and condemned us and made us "sharers with him in the gifts with which he has been endowed."

John Calvin, Institutes of the Christian Religion, 3.XI.10.

(ii) New life brings a new lifestyle. We who are in Christ have been, and are being, transformed by the Spirit. "...you have taken off your old self with its practices and have put on the new self, which is being renewed in knowledge in the image of its Creator" (Col 3:9-10). This call to mortification and vivification has profound implications for what we do with and to our bodies, for the Christian's body is now a temple of the Holy Spirit. "You are not your own;" says Paul, "you were bought at a price. Therefore honour God with your bodies" (1 Cor 6:19-20).

(iii) Among the vices of the old self that are to be discarded are envy and deception. I mention these particular sins because of their relevance to the subject at hand. Many who struggle with gender dysphoria are sorely tempted to covet a body other than the one they've been given. That is envy. The aim of those who seek to transition is to "pass" as being the opposite sex to what they, in fact, are. This is deception. Consequently, faithfulness to Christ cannot be separated from how a person manages their gender dysphoria. Such sins must be 'put off.'

(iv) This brings us to the virtues that believers are called to 'put on.' Four that are of especial relevance to our subject are patience, endurance, joy and thanksgiving.

> **Col 1:10-12**
> ...so that you may live a life worthy of the Lord and please him in every way... being strengthened with all power according to his glorious might so that you may have great endurance and patience, and giving joyful thanks to the Father, who has qualified you to share in the inheritance of his holy people in the kingdom of light.

Patience and endurance are vital for sufferers of gender dysphoria, particularly for those whose cross-gender identification is strong and persists over time. However, resistance and obedience are possible, although much prayer is needed that strength be given to this end. But, more than that, joy and thanksgiving are also possible – if not for the affliction itself, for the fruit suffering bears under the sovereign hand of God (Rom 5:3-5; Jam 1:2-4).

(v) Fifth, such a battle should never be fought alone. We need one another not only to keep each other accountable, but also to bear one another's burdens.

> **Gal 6:1-2**
> Brothers and sisters, if someone is caught in a sin, you who live by the Spirit should restore that person gently. But watch yourselves, or you also may be tempted. Carry each other's burdens, and in this way you will fulfil the law of Christ.

But what counts as 'transgression' and what counts as a 'burden'? In my view, the experience of gender incongruence clearly falls in the latter category. Mark Yarhouse is, therefore, right that "there is a need for the church to be able to cope with the disclosure of gender dysphoria among those who experience it and have the courage to share what they are going through."

Mark A. Yarhouse, *Understanding Gender Dysphoria: Navigating Transgender Issues in a Changing Culture* (Downers Grove: IVP, 2015), 151.

But, as we've seen, there are ways of managing gender dysphoria that fall squarely into the category of 'transgression'. What, then, will gentle restoration look like when such transgressions take place? No doubt a range of factors will need to be considered (e.g., age, maturity, and other mental health issues). Nevertheless, I cannot agree with Yarhouse that some believers "may benefit from space to find ways to identify with aspects of the opposite sex, as a way to manage extreme discomfort." Just because a person desires 'space' doesn't mean it is good for them. The good of the church must also be taken into account. Paul's concern – "a little yeast leavens the whole batch of dough" (1 Cor 5:6) – clearly has some application here.

Mark A. Yarhouse, "Understanding the Transgender Phenomenon."

compassion without compromise

3.5. Bodily resurrection and the life to come

The final piece of scriptural teaching relevant to our subject has to do with what is revealed about the nature of our resurrection bodies. Whilst there are all kinds of things we cannot know on this score (1 Cor 15:35-36), the Bible affirms a principle of both continuity and transformation: it is *these earthly bodies* that will be raised, but with *different qualities and capacities* (1 Cor 15:42-44). As Paul says, Christ "will transform our lowly bodies so that they will be like his glorious body" (Phil 3:21).

Curiously, the prospect of transformation has led some to speculate that we will be raised as either androgynous or monosexual or asexual beings. Given that our bodies are sexed in this world, and that the risen Jesus remains a man, it would require a very clear statement of Scripture to create the expectation that we will be raised as something other than eternally sexed (and therefore gendered) beings. But no such statement exists.

The only passage that could possibly be thought to suggest such a thing is Matthew 22:30 (and parallels): "At the resurrection people will neither marry nor be given in marriage; they will be like the angels in heaven." But while this passage clearly affirms that marriage belongs to this age only, it says nothing about the elimination of human sexual distinctions. In fact, Jesus' choice of words implies quite the opposite: as Augustine saw, "neither do they marry" can only refer to males and "nor are they given in marriage" can only apply to females.

<aside>Augustine, *The City of God*, 19.22.17.</aside>

Therefore, Scripture gives us no reason to doubt and every reason to believe that we will be resurrected as sexed (and therefore gendered) beings.

This glorious prospect has two implications. First, whilst we should be willing to spend and be spent in the cause of our Master, we are nonetheless to love our bodies. Indeed, says Paul, "no one ever hated their own body, but they feed and care for their body, just as Christ does the church" (Eph 5:29). Consequently, self-rejection and self-mutilation are not only tragic but also sinful. Those in Christ must, therefore, resist such temptations and instead fly to the throne of grace, where we can "receive mercy and find grace to help us in our time of need" (Heb 4:16).

Second, in the resurrection every form of disease and disorder will be healed and banished forever. In fact, so wonderful will be the glory revealed both to us and in us that the sufferings of this present time will not be worth comparing to it (Rom 8:18). This is good news, particularly for those whose gender dysphoria proves irresolvable in this life. Christians have a real hope that will not disappoint. This is why we must fix our eyes not on what is seen but on what is unseen (2 Cor 4:18).

4. CONCLUSION

In light of the Bible's teaching, the only conclusion possible is that gender dysphoria is one of the tragic effects of the fall. Furthermore, in the absence of any clear scientific evidence for regarding gender dysphoria as a type of intersex condition, it is best regarded as a psychiatric or psychological disturbance.

This, of course, doesn't remove the distress of those who suffer gender dysphoria. But it does lay some important foundations upon which to build a biblically informed and medically responsible pastoral approach. It likewise provides a helpful interpretive lens through which we can make sense of the various social, political and ideological changes going on around us. For not only is the basic assumption of transgender ideology false but the goal of transitioning is unrealisable. "Transgendered men do not become women, nor do transgendered women become men."

See Paul McHugh, "Transgenderism: A Pathogenic Meme", June 10th, 2015, online: www.thepublicdiscourse.com/2015/06/15145

What then is our message to those who have sought to transition? Two responses are in order. First, in our evangelism, we must not let the temporary overshadow the eternal. The greatest need of those who experience gender dysphoria or identify as transgender is not for their identity issues to be resolved (as wonderful as that would be), or their attempts at transition reversed (which may not be entirely possible), but to be reconciled to God and adopted as his children. In other words, like the rest of us, the transgendered and gender dysphoric need the gospel of Jesus Christ. For only in Christ can true hope be found and lasting peace known (John 14:27).

Second, whilst we come to Jesus as we are, he does not leave us as we are. His goal is to restore us and teach us to walk in a manner worthy of the Lord (Col 1:10). This will necessarily entail living, as far as is possible, in conformity with our God-given sex. For those who have gone down the path of transitioning, this will mean ceasing cross-hormone therapy, cross-dressing and other forms of cross-gender identification. Some surgical steps will, of course, be irreversible. If so, as Russell Moore argues, the person may need to see themselves akin to a biblical eunuch; that is, as one wounded physically by past sin, but awaiting wholeness in the resurrection. Whatever the case, strong pastoral care and congregational support will be essential.

Russell Moore, "Joan or John? My Answer: Part Two (May 26, 2009), online: www.russellmoore.com/2009/05/26/joan-or-john-my-answer-part-two

Finally, how should Christians respond to the transgender tsunami that is sweeping the western world? If we truly love our neighbours, we will not withdraw from the public square. We will pray fervently and, where possible, agitate politically for a more responsible and coherent therapeutic approach to the treatment of gender dysphoria and truly 'safer' school education programmes for all children. This may not always make us popular, but we dare not be silent. Our task, as Francis Schaeffer was want to say, is to present the truth with compassion but without compromise. P

the doctor will see you now

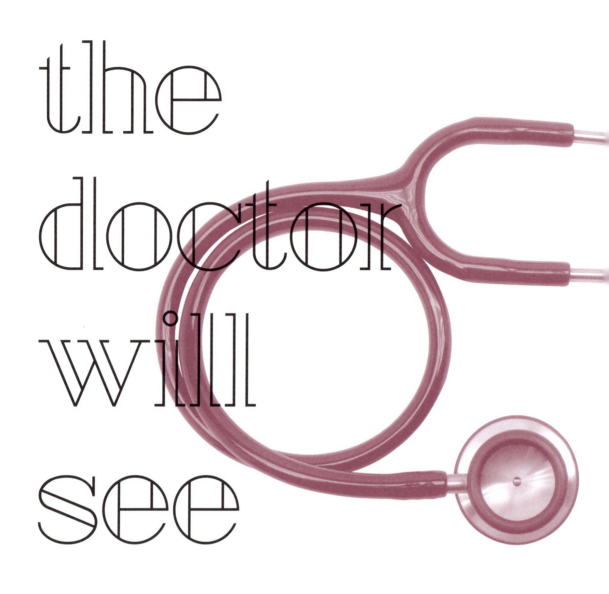

Still got questions? We thought it'd be a good idea to ask Dr Peter Saunders about the medical side of things.

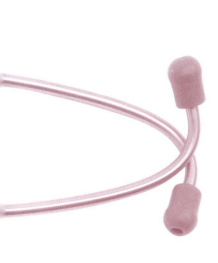

Until 2013, people were diagnosed with "gender identity disorder," but that has now changed to "gender dysphoria." What's the significance of the change?

Popular culture, law, politics and medicine have all changed how they deal with the issue of transsexuality.

Transsexuality was previously classified as 'gender identity disorder' by the medical profession. In other words, it was seen as a mental health condition.

However, in response to changes in culture and medical thinking the term 'gender identity disorder' in the DSM IV (Diagnostic and Statistical Manual of Mental Disorders, 4th Edition, 2000) was changed to 'gender dysphoria' in the DSM V (2013). Under the new term 'gender dysphoria' the condition is only thought to be a mental disorder when it causes distress to the individual. Otherwise it is viewed as a normal variant. The World Health Organisation (WHO) is now seeking to remove it from the category of mental disorder altogether.

The fundamental question is this: "How do we best help people experiencing incongruence between their body and their felt identity?" Should we alter the body to conform to a person's gender identity or beliefs, through hormones or transgender surgery? Or, alternatively, should we attempt to change a person's identity or beliefs to conform to the body, through counselling or psychotherapy? Or should we simply support the person in their conflicted state?

Although no analogy is perfect, some people have drawn a helpful parallel between gender dysphoria and the mental disorder anorexia nervosa. Both are conditions where there is incongruence between a person's beliefs and their biology. Both conditions also can cause huge distress and can prove very difficult to manage. But if we would not prescribe dieting or liposuction to someone with anorexia, then neither should we refer transgender people for hormone or surgical treatment, even if they desperately desire it.

But in choosing not to encourage people in the direction of taking irrevocable steps to change gender, we also need to recognise the confusing complexity of the conflict being experienced. This will involve offering acceptance, community and compassion in working with the affected person to find the least possible invasive ways to manage their dysphoria all the time pointing them to the One in whose image they are made and in whom real wholeness is found.

the doctor will see you now

How common is gender dysphoria?

Zucker KJ et al. Gender Dysphoria in Adults. *Annual Review of Clinical Psychology*, 2016 (18 January Epub ahead of print).

True gender dysphoria is very rare, involving fewer than one in 10,000 adult males and fewer than one in 30,000 adult females. However, gender dysphoria may be increasing in frequency judging by the number of people self-identifying or referring themselves to gender identity clinics.

This may be the result of transsexuality becoming more publically acceptable or may result from changes in family structures and therefore the environment in which children are growing up. The answer is not yet certain and may be resolved by further research.

What causes gender dysphoria?

neurodevelopmental: A disorder of brain function that affects emotion, learning ability and self-control and that unfolds as the individual grows.

psychosocial: Related to the psychological and social environment in which a child grows up.

The mechanisms leading to transsexuality are incompletely understood but genetic, neurodevelopmental and psychosocial factors probably all contribute. Various theories exist and, as in the debate about homosexuality, their proponents tend to favour either nature (biology) or nurture (upbringing). Given the breadth of the transgender umbrella, one unifying theory that would account for every case seems unlikely. It may well be that the causes are multifactorial and the combinations come from both nature and nurture. Good research, unbiased interpretation, open discussion and humility are all to be desired in seeking to grow greater understanding.

Is gender dysphoria associated with other medical problems?

Gender dysphoria in adults is associated with a variety of mental health problems. People with the condition are more likely to suffer from mood disorders, anxiety disorders and suicidal thoughts and actions. A major review of 38 cross-sectional and longitudinal studies has shown levels of psychopathology and psychiatric disorders (mental health problems) higher than the non-trans population.

In the US, suicide attempts among trans men and trans women are roughly ten times the rate found in the overall population. In Canada, in the province of Ontario, the suicide attempt rate amongst transgender people was about 18 times higher than the general population. The majority of studies show that the level of distress felt by people with gender dysphoria lessens after hormonal and surgical treatment. However, in 25% the outcome of surgery is not positive and does not solve their mental health difficulties.

What treatments are available for people who want to transition and what do they accomplish?

People who experience gender dysphoria will make a number of choices about how to manage it. Some choose to live in accordance with their biological sex and gender and learn ways of coping with the internal conflict that this creates for them.

Some will engage in cross-gender behaviour (such as cross-dressing) either intermittently or permanently and either publicly or in private.

Some will choose to adopt the cross-gender role through taking hormone treatment. So for example a man taking female hormones will develop female secondary sex characteristics such as breast enlargement, a higher voice and a female distribution of body hair. Or alternatively a woman taking male hormones will develop a deeper voice, changes in body shape, and male distribution of body hair.

Others may proceed to sex reassignment surgery. For a man wishing to transition to a woman this involves removal of the penis and testicles and fashioning of a vagina (vaginoplasty). For a person transitioning in the opposite direction the vagina is closed and a penis is created surgically from other bodily tissue (phalloplasty). Normally male to female surgery can be achieved in one step whereas female to male surgery is more complicated and may require up to four separate surgical procedures. Female to male surgery is more complex, more expensive and carries more complications. Surgical fashioning of external genitalia, however, will not bestow fertility. A trans woman cannot produce eggs and trans man cannot produce sperm.

How easy are these treatments to access currently?

A person presenting to their GP with gender dysphoria can be referred to a specialist clinic, such as the Tavistock and Portman NHS Trust Gender Identity Development Service in London. There they will be seen by specialists who may recommend hormone and/or surgical treatment. Currently these treatments are paid for on the NHS.

There are comprehensive 'good practice' guidelines drawn up by the Royal College of Psychiatrists for the assessment and treatment of adults with gender dysphoria. These provide guidance about hormone therapy, family support, hair treatment, speech and language therapy and genital surgery, and have received endorsement from most of the Medical Royal Colleges.

What practical concerns are there?

Changing a person's legal identity under the Gender Recognition Act (2004) allows transgender people to be legally recognised in their "new" gender. However, it doesn't require any change to their fundamental biology. In other words a man identifying as female may obtain a gender recognition certificate without having hormone treatment or surgery and so may look fully male.

Giving drugs to delay puberty, or hormones to change appearance, especially to children or young adolescents, may well affect brain development, bone growth, and fertility. If a doctor does not know that his or her patient was born male or female it may also mean diagnoses are missed.

For example, a woman who has had male hormones and genital surgery can still develop cancer of the uterus and cervix because she still has a womb. These cancers may prove very difficult to detect given that she will no longer have a vagina. In the same way a man who has had female hormones and genital surgery will still have a prostate and can still develop prostate cancer.

What are the implications for Christian doctors?

Most Christian doctors will feel extremely uncomfortable about prescribing hormones for patients suffering from gender dysphoria or referring them for gender reassignment surgery. At present the General Medical Council permits a doctor to exercise freedom of conscience "not to provide or refer any patient (including patients proposing to undergo gender reassignment) for particular services to which he or she may hold conscientious objection."

'Personal beliefs and medical practice,' online: www.gmc-uk.org/guidance

So, Christian doctors need not be involved in gender reassignment. However, they still need to make a decision about whether they should see patients presenting with gender dysphoria, whether they will refer them to a gender identity clinic and, if not, what support and care they can offer instead. There can be a huge amount of pressure placed upon doctors both by patients and colleagues to force them to be involved in treatment which they feel is not only medically inappropriate but also morally wrong. P

Finding Our Feet in Shifting Sands

Gender identity in the classroom and the courtroom

by Sharon James

Ryland is a little girl, now aged eight. As soon as she could talk, she claimed to be a boy and so her family concluded that she was transgender. They cut her hair, dressed her as a boy, and always used masculine pronouns. Aged just six, Ryland spoke at a diversity event in California, referring to herself as the "brother" of sister Brynly.

 My name is Ryland Michael Whittington. I'm a transgender kid. I am six. I am a cool kid. I am the happiest I have ever been.

BBC Newsbeat, "I am six and I'm a transgender kid. I am a cool kid" (3 June 2014), online: www.bbc.co.uk/newsbeat

Such cases appear in the media more and more frequently. Many of us will find this unsettling, in part because they are usually presented as 'good news' stories, and in part because of a growing sense that questioning such claims is unacceptable, offensive even.

So how should we respond? That's the question this article seeks to answer with an emphasis on public policy and education. We will look at what the dominant cultural view is (gender identity theory), then look at how that is shaping public policy and educational materials in UK schools, before offering some advice on how to respond as parents and youth workers.

1. WHAT IS GENDER IDENTITY THEORY?

The *Yogyakarta Principles* define gender identity as follows:

> *Gender identity is understood to refer to each person's **deeply felt internal and individual experience** of gender, which may or may not correspond with the sex assigned at birth, including the **personal sense of the body** (which may involve, if freely chosen, modification of bodily appearance or function by medical, surgical or other means) and other expressions of gender, including dress, speech and mannerisms.*

The *Yogyakarta Principles* were composed at an international conference in Java, Indonesia, in 2006 and published in Geneva in 2007. They lay out principles on the application of international human rights law in relation to "sexual orientation and gender identity" to be implemented by national governments. The principles are non-binding.

Note that gender identity is self-defined here. Everyone, it is claimed, has the right to be accepted by others in the gender identity they choose to present, based on their subjective sense of themselves, and divorced from any necessary connection with biological sex. Internal experience trumps what is presented as the arbitrary assignation of biological sex at birth. The terminology here is crucial: there is no sense of a physical reality that is recognised at birth (anatomical sex). Rather, assignation evokes a picture of a midwife dreaming up a random sex label and inscribing it on the unsuspecting infant.

This view of gender has a number of implications:

- In general, there is mounting pressure on all of us to accept people on the basis of their "deeply felt internal and individual experience", and their "personal sense of the body".

- This "deeply felt experience" becomes a sufficient reason to be awarded a change in legal status.

- There are increasing demands for access to spaces designated as women-only or men-only for anyone who identifies with that sex, regardless of their bodily attributes or appearance.

A number of Christians have challenged these claims, and so too have many non-Christians. Some feminists deny that a man can become a woman simply by claiming to be so, as do some free speech campaigners such as Brendan O'Neill. But gender identity theory, which even ten years ago was largely confined to academic discussion, has, it seems overnight, become mainstream and is being increasingly integrated into our legal and educational systems.

See for example, Albert R Mohler, *We Cannot Be Silent* (Nashville: Nelson Books, 2015).

Ensuring Fairness is a website expressing the views of feminists opposed to transgender claims, see *ensuringfairness.wordpress.com*; Germaine Greer, *The Whole Woman* (London: Doubleday, 1999), 64-74.

See for example, Brendan O'Neill, "Thou Shalt Not Take Caitlyn Jenner's Name in Vain", *Spiked* (3 June 2015).

2. WHAT IS THE CURRENT PUBLIC POLICY?

The Gender Recognition Act 2004 permits transsexual people who are over the age of eighteen, and who have lived in their assumed sex for at least two years, to apply to the Gender Recognition Panel for a Gender Recognition Certificate (GRC). Applicants need to provide a medical referral, but do not need to have undergone hormonal or surgical treatment. A GRC entitles someone to live "for all purposes" (including marriage) in their acquired sex. They are able to apply for a new birth certificate, indicating their new legal sex and name. The original birth certificate, although still existing, does not have to be disclosed. It is an offence in certain situations for someone to disclose a transsexual person's birth sex, with fines of up to £5,000.

Gender Recognition Act 2004, Sections 1(1), 2(1)(b) and 3(1).

Gender Recognition Act 2004, Section 9(1). At the time of the 2004 Act (which was passed before the recognition of same-sex marriages), full certificates were available for unmarried people. Married people had to apply for an interim certificate. If their marriage was subsequently ended they were entitled to a full certificate. A female to male transsexual person would be allowed to marry a woman once the full certificate had been obtained; similarly a male to female would be allowed to marry a male. Transsexuals who wished to continue in partnership with a previous spouse had to have their marriage annulled, and then enter a civil partnership as this would now be a same-sex partnership (for instance, a female to male, might wish to continue with their previous husband).

Gender Recognition Act 2004, Section 22. The offence relates to someone who has learned of the person's transition in an official capacity. There are exceptions, including a partial exception for church officials – see Gender Recognition (Disclosure of Information) (England, Wales and Northern Ireland) (No 2) Order 2005.

The Equality Act 2010 includes gender reassignment as a "protected characteristic", in the same way as race or religion. People who have a GRC are legally protected from discrimination (for example in the provision of goods and services), and harassment. In 2013 the Marriage (Same Sex Couples) Act made it possible for a marriage to continue following one spouse's legal transition, provided the other spouse agreed.

finding our feet in shifting sands

In January 2016, the House of Commons Women and Equalities Committee published the report *Transgender Equality*. Recommendations to the Government include:

- Those applying for a Gender Recognition Certificate should not have to seek authorisation from a doctor;
- Changing sex should be a quick and simple administrative change;
- In the future, as much documentation as possible should not require declaration of sex;
- Young people aged 16 and 17 should be able to change sex;
- It should be easier for children to access hormones to block puberty.

Transgender Equality: First Report of Session 2015-2016, House of Commons, Women and Equalities Committee, HC 390 (14 January 2016) 79-80, 84-86.

The Government published a response to these recommendations in July 2016, promising a new action plan for transgender equality, and, significantly, agreeing with the recommendation that gender dysphoria should not be classed as a mental illness.

Government Response to the Women and Equalities Committee Report on Transgender Equality, Government Equalities Office (July 2016), 5, 18.

3. WHAT IS BEING TAUGHT IN SCHOOLS?

There is no statutory requirement to teach children about transsexual issues, and hence the situation differs widely across the country. To give some idea of scale though, this year about 38,000 school children took part in UK Diversity Week, organised by the charity Just Like Us, with the aim of making "schools better places for LGBTQ+ pupils."

Christian Concern, "'LGBT Diversity Week' launched in schools", online: www.christianconcern.com

There are a plethora of other organisations offering advice to schools, especially under the umbrella of anti-bullying policies, and some schools are using resources which present a strongly trans-affirming worldview.

For example, the LGBT lobby group Stonewall has been given Government funding to combat bullying and promote tolerance in schools. Stonewall's booklet, *Getting Started: A toolkit for preventing and tackling homophobic, biphobic and transphobic bullying in primary schools*, includes a page of child-friendly explanations like this:

Government Equalities Office and the Department for Education Press Release, *Awards announced from £2 million homophobic bullying fund* (24 March 2015).

Getting Started: A toolkit for preventing and tackling homophobic, biphobic and transphobic bullying in primary schools, Stonewall (2016) 4, available online.

Gender Identity: *Everyone has a gender identity. This is the gender that someone feels they are. This might be the same as the gender they were given as a baby, but it might not. They might feel like they are a different gender, or they might not feel like a boy or a girl.*

Pronoun: *Words we use to refer to people's gender in conversation – for example, 'he' or 'she'. Some people may prefer others to refer to them in gender neutral language and use pronouns such as they / their and ze / zir.*

In similar fashion, the Department of Health funded a 2007 booklet which simply assumed gender identity theory:

Before we start, it is important to understand that sex is between the legs and gender is between the ears. Sex is... to do with your chromosomes, genitalia, hormones etc. Gender is... to do with your internal sense of self and how you choose to express yourself.

A guide for young trans people in the UK, Department of Health (2007), 4.

The advocacy and education group Gendered Intelligence helps children and young people understand this distinction by illustrating it visually with a cartoon figure. There is an arrow towards the lower part of the figure with the word 'sex' in capitals. Another arrow going between the ears has the word 'gender' in capitals, with the caption 'emotions, personality' in brackets. Lesson learned: sex and gender are totally different. You can choose and change gender whenever you want.

Trans Youth Sexual Health Booklet, Gendered Intelligence, 2, available online.

The support group Mermaids provides resources for schools which promote the idea of gender fluidity. The Gender Identity Research and Education Society (GIRES) has produced detailed guidelines which they offer to schools. These advise, for example, that schools should ensure that toilets and changing facilities are "immediately available in line with new gender presentation, and the young person's wishes."

www.mermaidsuk.org.uk/resources-for-professionals.html

Transition of a Pupil in School, GIRES (2015). In the GIRES guidelines to schools about teachers transitioning, schools are told that toilets and changing rooms must be made available to people in their new presenting sex: "If others do not wish to share the 'ladies' or 'gents' facilities with a trans person, then it is they, not the trans person, who must use alternative facilities." *Transition of a Teacher in School*, GIRES (June 2015), 8. See www.gires.org.uk/assets/Schools for both documents.

Educate & Celebrate, another LGBT support and advocacy organisation, delivers "LGBT+Inclusive training to staff, support staff, departments, leadership teams and governors in children's centres, nurseries, primary and secondary schools, colleges, universities and public and private organisations." Their *PRIDE in Early Years Education* is a range of picture books, activities and lesson plans to help make children's centres and nursery schools LGBT+Friendly. Educate & Celebrate present gender identity as male, female or other, each on a spectrum, independent of the sex assigned at birth. Birmingham City Council (in its role as the Local Authority) has arranged for Educate & Celebrate staff training and assembly resources to be available in all its schools.

'Training', *Educate & Celebrate*, online: www.educateandcelebrate.org/training-2

Trans+ Tips for Teachers, Educate & Celebrate, available on their website.

'Training and Policy', *Birmingham City Council*, online: www.birmingham.gov.uk/downloads/file/3381/educate_and_celebrate

finding our feet in shifting sands

A new educational resource produced by LGBT activists and funded by the Government Equalities Office, *Inspiring Equality in Education*, provides a series of detailed primary and secondary lesson plans which teach pupils that their biological sex is just a label. The only thing that limits their gender expression is their imagination. The activist group Educational Action Challenging Homophobia (EACH) produces educational resources, including a video that explains gender identity to students. It features several students who testify that they have found freedom in asserting their own, self-defined identity, and urging others to do the same.

See www.each.education/schools-and-colleges/inspiring-equality-in-education

Inspiring Equality In Education, Educational Action Challenging Homophobia, 2016, page 3.35, online: www.each.education/wordpress2/wp-content/uploads/2016/05/EACH_secondary-lesson-plans_may.pdf

See "What is Gender? (Inspiring Equality in Education)," EACH, 31 March 2016, online: www.youtube.com/watch?v=qlYtj0sf6ec

In 2015, Turnham Primary School asked parents and children to sign a "home-school agreement." Children as young as three were asked to sign a commitment that they would:

> *Be tolerant of others whatever their race, colour, gender, class, ability, physical challenge, faith, sexual orientation or lifestyle and refrain from using racist or homophobic or transphobic language in school.*

Peter McKay, "Warped logic of trying to brainwash three-year-olds," *Mail Online* (27 April 2015).

That, of course, means that these young children will need to be told what "transphobic language" is. Indeed this is crucial, given the way in which so much of this educational material is promoted in order to combat transphobia. Often definitions will speak about the hatred or rejection of transsexual people, and of course Christians must oppose that kind of transphobia. But the definition offered by the charity Galop is considerably broader:

> *Transphobia is intolerance of gender diversity. It is based around the idea that there are only two sexes – male or female, which you stay in from birth.*

'What is Transphobia?,' Galop, online: www.galop.org.uk/transphobia/what-is-transphobia

Note that here disagreement with gender identity theory is equated with intolerance, which is equated with phobia. The clear implication is that it is hateful to disagree with gender identity theory.

In light of all this, it is important for parents to ask questions, to familiarise themselves with resources that are being used in their child's school, and be aware of visiting organisations. All discussion with schools should of course be conducted in a courteous and constructive way, but parents have the legal right to find out what is taught in sex education lessons, and it may be possible to suggest alternative input. Beyond that, though, how else should we respond?

The Christian Institute has a dedicated Education Officer who can offer advice if needed.

4. HOW SHOULD WE RESPOND?

A. Hold on to the truth

There is huge pressure from the culture, and even from within the evangelical church, to accept and affirm individuals' own claims about their identity, especially if they are clearly suffering deep anguish. But, as in every pastoral interaction, true compassion has to be grounded in God's good design for humanity. Our Creator has revealed his will for human flourishing. Testimonies from those who transition and then, sometimes many years later, regret it, point to the false compassion of affirming transition. They agree that when someone in the church affirmed their transition, it provided the euphoria of acceptance. Yet, deep down, peace with God was not going to be found until truth was confronted. So we need to help young people to see that holding onto the truth in this and every area is the most compassionate response.

Some helpful testimonies can be found in Shick, D (Ed.) *Understanding Gender Confusion*, Help4Families (2014). See also *Sex Change Regret* (*sexchangeregret.com*) a website for support of those who have transitioned and later regret it.

We can also help them to challenge the assumptions of gender identity theory. Do we really have to accept what people think in their minds that they are? How far must this go? Age? Race? One could discuss with young people the widely circulated short film of interviews with students at Washington University, where the imperative to accept such claims is exposed as defying rationality.

'College Kids Say the Darndest Things: On Identity', Family Policy Institute of Washington, 13 April 2016, online: *www.youtube.com/watch?v=xfO1veFs6Ho*

B. Resist pressure to affirm early social transition or medical treatment

Children are being diagnosed with gender dysphoria at a younger and younger age. In the past year, three pre-school children and a total of 167 children under the age of ten were referred to the Gender Identity Service at the Tavistock and Portman Clinics in London and Leeds.

Steve Doughty, "Children aged three get transgender therapy on NHS: Pre-school infants among 167 youngsters aged 10 or under who received treatment last year," *Mail Online*, 4 May 2016. In 2015 the Tavistock and Portman Trust reported a four-fold increase in children under ten reporting 'gender confusion' since 2009-2010. In 2009-2010 there were 19 under-11s referred; in 2014-15 there were 77. See Laura Donnelly, "Rise in child transgender referrals," *The Telegraph* (7 April 2015).

finding our feet in shifting sands

There is vigorous debate about what is the appropriate treatment for children diagnosed in this way. Some people advocate supporting a complete social transition to live as members of the opposite sex (change of name, pronouns, clothing, hairstyle, use of facilities of the opposite sex, etc.). Others would advocate prescription of puberty suppression drugs (hypothalamic hormone suppression at ages 10-13) as a means of making sex reassignment less traumatic in later adolescence.

Hembree W C, Cohen-Kettenis P, Delemarre-van de Waal H A et al, 'Endocrine Treatment of Transsexual Persons: An Endocrine Society Clinical Practice Guideline', *Journal of Clinical Endocrinology & Metabolism*, 94(9) (September 2009), 3138.

However, all of these are to be resisted. Advice presented by the Endocrine Society Clinical Practice Guideline on the treatment of transsexuals recommends against the social transitioning of pre-puberty children. One of the reasons for that, and for avoiding hormone treatments, is that in the great majority of cases, when children claim to be "in the wrong body", if they are left alone, in time, their experience of gender dysphoria resolves itself. Of course, the challenge remains as to how to help those who do not, but many would maintain that to intervene medically is unnecessary and unwise.

According to DSM-V, as many as 98% of 'gender confused' boys and 88% of 'gender confused' girls eventually accept their biological sex after naturally passing through puberty. *Diagnostic and Statistical Manual of Mental Disorders, Fifth Edition*, American Psychiatric Association (Arlington, VA: 2013), 451-459 (specifically page 455).

Paul McHugh, "Transgender Surgery Isn't the Solution," *The Wall Street Journal* (June 12 2014). For medical risks of hormone treatment see Phelan, J E, 'Dangers of Hormone Treatments', in Shick, D (Ed.) *Understanding Gender Confusion* (Help4Families, 2014), 20-24. See also the chapter 'Transgender Children' in Heyer, W, *Paper Genders: Pulling the Mask Off the Transgender Phenomenon* (Make Waves Publishing, 2011), 25-45.

C. Oppose unnecessary stereotypes and bullying

We need to recognise that some stereotypes are cultural, not biblical.

Just because a little boy is unusually artistic and gentle does not mean that he should be pushed into thinking of himself as homosexual or transgender. A little girl may be sporty and tomboyish, but that doesn't mean that she should be pushed into identifying as lesbian or trans.

Anecdotally, it seems that behaviours that would have been accepted as within the normal range even a few years ago (girls wanting to play boys' games and dress in a tomboyish way, or boys wanting to play with dolls, etc.) are now being interpreted as gender confusion. This defies common-sense, and plays into what have, for years, been criticised as rigid and unhelpful stereotypes of what it means to be a boy or a girl.